Favourite Watering Holes

Favourite Watering Holes

Featuring pubs in
north and mid Wales

IAN PARRI

First published in 2008
Based on Ian Parri's column in the *Daily Post*

© Text: Ian Parri
© Photographs: *Daily Post*/Gwasg Carreg Gwalch

ISBN: 978-1-84524-128-5

Published by
Llygad Gwalch,
Ysgubor Plas, Llwyndyrys,
Pwllheli, Gwynedd, Wales, LL53 6NG.
Tel: 01758 750432
www.carreg-gwalch.com

INDEX

INTRODUCTION

FOR more years than he'll care to remember, Ian Parri has been one of Wales' foremost chroniclers, his travels in pursuit of the stories behind the news giving him ample opportunity to sample, in between times, the wares of the country's many and varied watering holes, good, bad or indifferent.

Based on this wealth of insight and experience, Ian has now gathered together, for the first time in this handy volume, fifty of his favourite pubs from throughout north and mid-Wales, whether ancient or modern, urban or rural, for the delectation of devotees and novices, locals and visitors alike, as originally written for the pages of north Wales' best loved newspaper.

Inside this book you'll discover what makes these hostelries so special. Enjoy!

Rob Irvine,
Editor, Daily Post

FOREWORD

WHILE Wales has often been painted as a chapel-going nation with barely a good word to be said for our pubs and inns, the reality is that our watering holes have lasted rather better than our houses of worship.

But we were never as "Bible-black" as Dylan Thomas made us out to be. It was always the case that a substantial number – probably the majority of our menfolk – still thronged to their local even at the height of the short-lived nonconformist religious revival of the early 20th century.

I was brought up in between these two factions, one of a family without much of a pub-going tradition, yet an individual who always found them hospitable and interesting places from an age when I probably shouldn't even have been darkening their doors.

I was possibly fated therefore to find employment first as a journalist, a tribe noted for its celebrated adherence to the pub culture, and later as a publican myself.

Now I find myself combining both roles, working as a columnist for the *Daily Post*, North Wales' premier daily paper, while with my wife Cath running the historic freehouse known as the Feathers Inn (www.tafarnyplu.com) in David Lloyd George's boyhood village of Llanystumdwy, near Cricieth.

We're fortunate in Wales in having a plethora of inns and pubs that are a living, breathing testimony to our nation's history and culture.

However the pubcos are working hard to subsume all this under a dung-heap of hegemony, in which they see all pubs as being identical entities, with identical plastic breweriana, identical beers and spirits and often identical menus.

In a weekly feature in the pages of the *Daily Post* I sought to celebrate my favourite pubs within the paper's circulation area in north and mid-Wales. They are precisely that – my favourite pubs.

They're chosen for a variety of reasons: ambience, location, history, reputation, quality of service, their Welsh ethos, and the hospitableness of their clientele and hosts. They're not all posh by any stretch of the imagination, just real pubs serving real people.

You might not have the same taste in pubs. I invite you to try them out all the same.

Ian Parri

BLACK BOY INN,
CAERNARFON

GASPS of shock reverberated from Rio to Rhosgadfan when owners, Welsh Historic Inns, announced it was to refurbish its most iconic pub. Surely not, they muttered in hushed but rebellious tones of horror, not another plastic revamp.

The Black Boy Inn, occasionally spelt as the Black Buoy, lies within Caernarfon's medieval town walls and has been a public house since 1522. Tipplers from throughout the globe have mis-spent hours of their youth, not to mention later life, within its sometimes chaotic confines.

To have visited Caernarfon but not to have popped into the "Black" is tantamount to being in Paris without seeing the Eiffel Tower. It's a *faux pas* not to be committed.

After all, its rickety furniture of unmatching pieces, its uneven floor, its scuffed doors, and the maze of narrow corridors leading to the toilets were as much part of its fabric as its colourful regulars and their even more colourful language.

But the traditionalists needn't have worried. The much-feared refurb actually embellished its medieval attraction. The regulars and their language, as colourful in Welsh as it is when an occasional aside is made in English, still throng here. As do the tourists. Shame, though, about the strictly 21st century blaring widescreen TV that seems to be permanently switched on.

Cool and dark beneath its low-slung black beamed ceilings, and within its thick stone walls, in winter the public bar is heated by open fires. The same goes for the rather more sedate lounge with its eclectic collection of chairs and tables that look like remnants from a bardic convention.

It's here that the more middle-aged huddle on Saturday nights, while in the teeming bar the stallions seek their mares, and vice versa, preparing for that 10.30pm gallop to the night-clubs.

But people of all ages happily seek refuge in each other's company, where even the most tongue-tied will find themselves drawn into the conversation.

Although you'll find a selection of cask ales on the bar, most locals cling to their pints of fizzy lager.

People happily chomp on their bar meals alongside others just there for the "hwyl" and the alcohol, with little elbow room for either. A sojourn in the quieter confines of the pub's separate restaurant better suit those of a less gregarious disposition.

The picnic tables on the pedestrianised Northgate Street outside prove popular long into the chilly dusk, with the gulls' aim seemingly improving as the sun recedes behind the mystical island of Anglesey.

The street shows little sign of its seedy past as a red light district in the town's heyday as a port.

It's said that the still-used original name of Stryd Pedwar a Chwech (Four and Six Street) derives from this time.

The politically correct insist it's because it cost four pence a night to sleep on the floor in the "Black", and six pence in a bed. Others say it's because it cost travellers four shillings and sixpence for a bed, a bottle of gin and a naughty lady's services. Either way, it's evidently always been a place of great colour.

Black Boy Inn, Caernarfon LL55 1RW. 01286 673604
www.welsh-historic-inns.com

BLACK LION INN,
DERWEN-LAS

THE ancient little tavern deserves better than to have its tartan-patterned carpet sullied by boots caked in glutinous mud, I think to myself as a group of walkers saunter in, the tallest of them having to retract his shoulders and crook his neck to get to the bar.

It is perhaps an over-reaction to suggest that a whack on the forehead, as he tries to traverse beneath the low-slung beamed ceiling, might be just what he deserves.

There are a number of intriguing wayside inns that have become enigmas as I've passed them down the years, burdened by indecent haste and unable to stop. The Black Lion in Derwen-las, just south of Machynlleth on the A487, has long since been on my must-do list.

And at last here I am, having gingerly pushed open the door and immediately found myself in a living museum of a pub, a little gem of a place. And just minutes after I've sat down to enjoy my sedentary survey of the place, able to see into virtually every nook and cranny from this vantage point, here I am tut-tutting at some customers' muddy thoughtlessness.

It's market day in Machynlleth just down the road. The pub is humming with low-key voices chattering over lunch in Welsh here, and in English over there, with the soothing classical music piped into the single room complementing the discourse rather than competing with it.

A couple of smartly-suited men look slightly out of place in such a rustic setting, where one almost expects to see shepherds' crooks standing to attention behind the door. They proceed to talk shop as they chin-wag over their salad and baked potato, wisely heeding a prominent notice on the bar beseeching patrons to turn off their mobile phones.

A huge crackling blaze fills the massive inglenook fireplace, logs at the ready by its side, drawing most diners to that side of the inn. The Black Lion has been here a very long time, since the mid-16th century in fact, and has always served the locality as an inn.

It seems difficult to believe now that it used to be a quayside tavern, once one of two – alongside its sister pub, the Tafarn Isaf, down the road – in this tiny hamlet.

Derwen-las, today seemingly totally landlocked and hemmed in by Montgomeryshire's emerald meadows, was in fact once a thriving port. Ships used to make their way here up the Dyfi, and jolly Jack Tars would have thronged to the bar to offload their tales of the high seas on disbelieving farmers.

Nowadays it caters just as much for those in need of food as it once did those seeking navy rum, and has created quite a name for itself as a purveyor of fine pub fare.

Don't make the same mistake I did: stop awhile rather than passing. And if you find a gangly walker with a lump on his forehead, try not to laugh out loud.

Black Lion Inn, Derwen-las SY20 8TN.
01654 703913

BLUE BELL INN,
HALKYN

TRUNDLING over the industrially pock-marked desolation of Halkyn Mountain, where some would have you believe King Arthur rests, the mist lifts temporarily to leave a stunning vista over the Dee and the Flintshire Bridge to some distant land.

My attention however is purloined by a squat building cradled by the mountainside, announced by a roadside sign telling me this is Y Gloch Las. Probably better known as the Blue Bell Inn, this is one of the north east's more intriguing public houses.

A kaleidoscope of new tongue tingling experiences, a session here should be a semester in any self-respecting drinker's education.

The rainbow of brewers' stripes on the empty casks by the door – marking which belongs to which brewery – should be ample pre-warning of the delights ahead. They tell only half the story.

Sure, you can whet your whistle on the pub's own specially brewed Blue Bell Bitter, or a host of other hand-pulled elixirs that'll include the prime of local brews from both sides of the border.

But in a deluded world from a marketing man's imagination which believes that Ireland is the centre of the cider-making world, it's so refreshing to be in a bar that knows its onions as far as alcoholic apple juice is concerned. Not to mention its pear-based cousin, known as perry before Marketing Man stupidly decided to call it pear cider for those without the nous to know that cider is exclusively made from apples.

Here you can tangle your tongue over the complex tastes of Welsh perry and exquisitely dry cider from Radnorshire, among a host of others from better known orchard-laden shires the other side of Offa's Dyke. Even Adam might have been tempted to indulge, in a cider drinker's own Garden of Eden. Little wonder that CAMRA has acknowledged it as its Regional Cider Pub of the Year.

The Blue Bell is a freehouse built in the mid-18th century, reputedly named after a local buccaneer's ship with which he used to plunder vast fortunes from other unfortunate seafarers. And while it's the taxman that spoils our little adventures these days, in his days it was the hangman. It's said that the pirate's remains are buried just down the road. Be grateful for small mercies as you fill in that tax return.

The pub, on the outskirts of Halkyn, offers a plethora of activities, from jazz, folk and plain old singalongs, to games nights, Welsh lessons and even walks over the mountain. The boot-cleaning paraphernalia consisting of broom heads plonked by the door indicate that this is a walkers' mecca, where tired feet are gratefully rested in front of the fire.

As for the food, they use organic vegetables from Northop, ice cream from Cheshire, and buffalo, pork and lamb bred almost in the next field.

Blue Bell Inn, Halkyn CH8 8DL.
01352 780309
www.bluebell.uk.eu.org

BRIGANDS' INN,
MALLWYD

A SEA of faces – mostly young – turn to see who's making a dripping entrance into their local through the driving rain this windswept Saturday night.

They smile and nod their welcomes, then return to whatever chit-chat had been occupying their thoughts. The place is a-hum with that distinctive dialect of Welsh they speak in these parts, in which vowels are taken as objects to be marvellously manipulated and twisted at will.

Thankfully the welcome is distinctly warmer than what might have awaited strangers back in the 16th century, when the feared Gwylliaid Cochion Mawddwy – the red-headed bandits of Mawddwy – ruled the roost around here.

It's said that this former coaching inn, sitting at a crossroads that has for centuries been one of the main interchanges for travellers going north-south (on what is now the A470) and east-west across mid-Wales, was one of their haunts.

It's certainly old enough and, although extensively revamped and renovated as recently as 2004, retains the moody and atmospheric atmosphere that marks a place of great antiquity.

It was originally known as the Peniarth Arms, ironically after the estate owned by the outlaws' arch-enemy Baron Lewis Owen's family, and later as Bury's Hotel.

It was re-named the Brigands' Inn towards the middle of the last century, in recognition of its links with a criminal fraternity still warmly thought of by many as warriors who fought the commoner's cause against the omnipotent gentry.

Over 80 of them were seized one Christmas Eve and later executed for their troubles by the Baron, the Sheriff of Meirionnydd.

But they got their own back on October 11, 1555, when they

ambushed him and his retinue and killed him at a spot just down the road towards Llangadfan still known as Llidiart y Barwn (the Baron's Gate). Obviously not people to tangle with.

There's still the odd hint of ginger on heads around the bar, but they seem affable enough these days, and I'm not tempted to feel for my scabbard.

Meanwhile a tidal wave of upper class chortling floods over from another bar, in complete contrast to the more down-to-earth company I'm keeping. I'm informed they're rich youngsters down from England for a spot of pheasant shooting, an important and extremely valuable part of this highly rural area's economic portfolio.

The Brigands' is a maze of rooms, featuring open timberwork and slate floors, all very tastefully renovated and offering several nooks and crannies for that private talk or even illicit smooch.

Catering for weddings and all sorts of functions, it naturally enough places great stock on its food offering. It boasts of its mix of contemporary and classic Welsh cuisine, and specialises in game and fish. And all without a bandit in sight.

Brigands' Inn, Mallwyd SY20 9HJ.
01650 511999
www.brigandsinn.com

BRONDANW ARMS,
LLANFROTHEN, NEAR PORTHMADOG

CERTAIN public houses have that certain alluring timeless quality. Not only has time stood still behind its welcoming doors, but thankfully continues to do so.

Any major move towards modernity would be sacrilege on a huge scale in any self-respecting innophile's eyes. The Brondanw Arms is one of those, a jewel not best suited to the needs of 21st century urban youth.

Leased from the Plas Brondanw estate up the road, once owned by Sir Clough Williams-Ellis, the architect behind the Italianate village of Portmeirion, it still pays tribute to the connection by being painted in the distinctive Portmeirion green – more of a turquoise in reality – concocted by Sir Clough.

Better known as Y Ring among the locals, with countless theories behind its nickname, to call at Llanfrothen's only pub is akin to popping back to one's own past, further even. It yells out for a jazz quartet plucking away languidly in the corner, or a pianist, as the ice clinks invitingly into another gin and tonic.

Yes, it does see its regular robust jamming sessions when local musicians turn up with fiddles and guitars to reel off all the old favourites. But it's as a venue for an altogether more modern brand of hoeing-on-downs that earns the place its kudos among the younger generation, who also seem to love its easy-going nature.

While it does have its ageing hippy element among the clientele, transplanted here from across the border, most of the locals could trace their roots back to when this flood valley up the Glaslyn from Porthmadog first silted up. It's the sort of community-based hostelry that screams for its proprietors to be imbued in the local culture, not least the lingo.

One of the Stockport-based Robinson's chain of pubs, Y Ring is a rambling place of huge character, dotted with memorabilia and paraphernalia. You're likely to encounter diners throughout the place, sitting wherever the fancy takes them.

It has acquired for itself a reputation as something of a food pub, but hasn't neglected its traditional drinkers either, many of whom travel from Porthmadog, Penrhyndeudraeth and beyond for its ambience as much as its beer.

To sit on one of the tree-shaded benches in the sliver of a front garden watching the meagre traffic trundle lazily up the road towards Cwm Croesor is a treat in itself. This is Provencal living with a distinctly Welsh twist.

To the rear lies extensive gardens, children's play area and oodles of parking space. It's very much a pub for the community, and whole families while away entire summer evenings out here in the back.

It regularly lays on live music in the extensive open lounge, while on international rugby days it transforms itself effortlessly into a passing resemblance of the Millennium Stadium's reverberating South Stand.

But most other times it dozes on with life like a contented cat that couldn't be bothered to look at a mouse let alone catch one.

Brondanw Arms,
Llanfrothen, near Porthmadog LL48 6AQ.
01766 770555
www.frederic-robinson.com

CANN OFFICE HOTEL,
LLANGADFAN

THERE can be few hostelries in Wales with a stranger sounding name than the Cann Office. Equally, there can be few places with a warmer welcome.

A real farmer's watering hole, it's wholly unpretentious, with the lilting sound of Montgomeryshire Welsh bubbling through its very fabric.

Yet it's equally popular in summer with the hordes of tourists either passing on their way between the English Midlands and the Cardigan Bay resorts, or staying in the caravan parks that pepper the area.

The kids love the extensive beer garden and its array of playground equipment, which includes a bouncing castle that falls flat as a pancake when the pump is switched off at dusk, much to the youngsters' consternation.

Those with the constitution for a heavy night might opt to stay in one of this ancient inn's six letting rooms, but should remember that the locals' noisy exuberance can last well into the night.

But back to its quirky name. It's been known as the Cann Office since at least 1795, but the roots of the name would seem to be rather more ancient. In fact it's believed to be derived from Cae'n y Ffos, meaning a fortified field, and 12th century earthworks near the rear of the hotel would certainly seem to give credence to this theory.

There's absolutely no doubt about the antiquity of the place, which once stood on a major drovers' road leading to the English markets, now metamorphosed as the A458. It was founded in 1310, and the first tenant was a certain Madoc ap Owen de Blowty.

It's said that the Franco-Welsh usurper of the English throne, Henry Tudor, stopped here on August 10th, 1485 while on his way to the Battle of Bosworth.

On entering through the front door, an interminably long corridor stretches out into the distance, bars and lounges flung either side. One is the ubiquitous pool room, but I'm intrigued to find the snug on my right is called the Cocktail Bar.

It's rather incongruous to think of these burly farmers shifting uncomfortably in their wellies as the barman twirls their favourite Sex On The Beach or Bloody Mary concoction behind his back.

While the bar-less lounge to the left boasts a piano, a rare commodity in today's juke-box oriented pubs, it's the slate-flagged public bar further along that's actually the real centre of musical excellence.

Nicknamed the Cut Lloi *(calf shed)* for its utilitarian, agricultural ambience, it has actually spawned its own concert party – Parti Cut Lloi – which performs throughout Wales and has its own albums in the record shops.

The Cann Office is also a bit of a honey-pot for those out for a spot of good old pub grub, with sirloin steak always a popular option.

Cann Office Hotel,
Llangadfan, Powys SY21 0PL.
01938 820202

DOUGLAS ARMS,
BETHESDA

"THAT'LL be £2.40", the lady behind the bar informs me as she places my pint of cider on the sliver of a counter formed out of one of several serving hatches surrounding the sizeable central servery.

So that's one abiding memory dashed, of when until fairly recent times landlord Geoff Davies would've told me in pounds, shillings and pence how much I owed.

Mind you, two pounds and eight shillings – written as £2/8/0 – does sound a heck of a lot for some crushed apples.

Still, it's the only tradition that seems to have fallen by the wayside in this fascinating old pub.

And the old mechanical till, which would've pinged triumphantly as Geoff Davies pressed those heavy buttons with gusto, still stands over there in the foyer as a tribute to bygone years. Thankfully, the place is still in the family's hands.

The whine of the wind howls through this rambling building, and the doors judder, on this blustery January night. There's neither a TV set nor juke box offering a hint of background noise to compete with Mother Nature's fierce tongue-lashing.

However a comforting hum of chatter seeps out of a cosy snug to the right, while somebody else is in deep conversation in another bar to the left of the staircase that sets off from the foyer – itself a popular place to sup – to the licensees' private accommodation.

To the left, served by its own hatch, lies the pub's games room, surrounded by staid leather benches and surprisingly fitted out with its own full-sized snooker table.

The place is illuminated by fluorescent light tubes strategically placed here and there, in a very definite throwback to the 1960s.

Meanwhile painted wooden shutters permanently rolled up above the bar hint at some attempts at what would've been seen as modernisation in the 1960s or 1970s. Precious little else, however, has changed down the decades. Even the shutters would probably now be seen as historical artefacts.

Little wonder that the Douglas Arms has for some years been included in the Campaign for Real Ale's Inventory of Historic Pub Interiors. And justifiably so.

And with only ten Welsh pubs out of the 3,000 still in existence having made their way onto the Inventory, it's an honour not to be sniffed at. A postscript on the certificate on the wall bluntly warns that its return might well be demanded if the property undergoes any significant changes.

Historians might be surprised to learn that the pub is named after the Douglas-Pennant regime that once ruled the local slate industry with an iron fist and little sympathy, and who in centuries past included human slavery in the Caribbean on their business portfolio.

Suffice to say that it once belonged to the family's Penrhyn estate, when to have named it anything else would've been tantamount to commercial suicide.

Douglas Arms, Bethesda LL57 3AY.
01248 600219

DUDLEY ARMS HOTEL,
LLANDRILLO

AT the supposed height of Methodist teetotalism, when having a quick drink was considered marginally worse than dancing the tango with the cloven-hoofed one, Llandrillo boasted seven public houses.

Ironically enough, as the passage of time has whittled down the number of chapels that bother to open their doors, the same fate has befallen our pubs. Llandrillo, a picturesque and quiet village near Corwen, now counts itself lucky to have maintained its solitary remaining pub – the Dudley Arms Hotel.

The jumble of outhouses that crowd menacingly around the car park at the back of the place illustrate that it was once also used as a farmhouse, an early example of agricultural diversification that no doubt helped save its bacon as an inn when all others faced financial ruin.

It once also boasted its own petrol pump, a common enough occurrence in rural hostelries at one time, as it sought to be all things to all men. Another important asset was the field behind, which hosted football competitions and sheep dog trials in its time.

Still very much a Welsh speaking pub, although it also hosts its share of tourists, the Dudley Arms remains an important focal point for the agricultural community.

I assume that two of its younger members are deeply engrossed in farm talk as they climb from their stools either end of the bar to devour generous platefuls of good honest pub food. The talk later revolves around a hog roast which is evidently part of some event or other being organised; the pub obviously is still the hub of activity in these parts.

The small front bar is very olde worlde, with various attempts at modernisation down the decades having failed to eradicate its character, even if the rest of the place does disappointingly show

26

evidence of a latter-day draughtsman's zeal for angular conformity.

However the lack of any background music in what is an eerily quiet place in the early evening like this can be quite unnerving, with chit-chats reduced to whispers that better belong in doctors' waiting rooms. I feel like reaching for a dog-eared copy of the *Reader's Digest*, if only there was one there.

The silence was doubtless due to a lack of bodies willing to shove their spare coins in the juke box, which includes a number of modern Welsh albums among its more international offerings.

We're instructed to avoid the tables adorned with place-mats if we've simply popped in for a drink, and we duly search for a simple bare table to plop our drinks on as we survey this ancient old place. If only these walls could talk.

Named after the land-owning Dudley dynasty that ruled the roost in these parts, it was taken over at the height of World War I by Owen Davies and his wife, who moved in from the Prince of Wales in nearby Cynwyd. The Davies family were to remain in charge here for 73 years, Roy Davies being the last in the lineage when he finally sold the place in 1990.

Dudley Arms,
Llandrillo, near Corwen LL21 0TL.
01490 440223
www.dudleyarms.co.uk

EAGLES INN,
LLANUWCHLLYN

THE chap behind the bar gets out his order pad and pencil almost as soon as we've shoved open the door, the first ones in the place at 6pm. Such is the good name harvested by the Eagles for its food that he obviously expects diners not drinkers at this time of evening.

Fresh Llyn Brenig trout screams at me off the specials board – being the lover of all things fishy that I am – to order it.

Sadly I have to turn a deaf ear to its piscine pleadings, as we have not long since eaten and need to be in Harlech by 7.30pm.

We sheepishly order a measly pint and a soft drink, but a quick perusal through the hefty home-cooked menu elicits a promise to return with rumbling stomachs and more time on our hands in the near future.

Having entered from the spacious car park, we find ourselves in a cavernous and comfortable, if somewhat nondescript and over-lit, lounge.

Doubling up as a dining room, it's also the functions room which hosts gigs, concerts and much of the social activity in this close-knit community on the opposite bank from Bala of Llyn Tegid, Wales' largest natural lake.

Feeling rather lonely within its echoing walls, we grasp our drinks and make our way to the public bar. It turns out to be far more rustic in ethos, probably the original section of the pub, and what one would expect of an establishment that dares add the embellishment "inn" to its name.

We've just had time to park our posteriors on one of the wooden settles that lean on the walls around the bar when the latch on the hefty door clicks to announce the arrival of more clientele, who order their drinks and settle down with a copy each of the menu.

The bar boasts low beams that a member of the Harlem Globetrotters might have problems with, a traditional low-maintenance slate floor, and an interesting inglenook fireplace in the corner. Another couple of people pop in, and settle down on stools by the bar.

But with a lack of any background music, the conversation around the bar is as muted as a vasectomy clinic's waiting room. However "Wales Today" blares away annoyingly on a spoilt brat of a tiny TV set, demanding attention.

Photographs of the village soccer team, which plays in the rather grandly-titled Welsh National League – which in effect serves Wrexham and parts of the north east – adorn the walls. Evidently the team's HQ, this serves as further evidence of the Eagles' role within the community.

The pub also benefits from being within shunting distance of the terminus and HQ of Rheilffordd Llyn Tegid, the narrow-gauge railway that chugs its way along the lakeside between here and Bala, and it's not unusual to see its uniformed volunteers popping in for a quick one. Anybody seen the Fat Controller, then?.

Eagles Inn, Llanuwchllyn, near Bala LL23 7UB.
01678 540278
www.eaglesinnbala.co.uk

GARDDFON INN,
Y FELINHELI

WITH the wind whipping up the brine off the tumultuous Menai Strait outside and pebble-dashing the windows with it, the Garddfon Inn couldn't help but have a maritime feel to it.

It almost feels like being cosily ensconced aboard a sea going vessel, and those of a queasy disposition might well feel the *mal-de-mere* rising before they put their first drink to their lips. Not me, though, guv'nor.

Doubtless, however towards, the end of the evening the floor would begin to sway in time to the waves spitting their venom against the inland promenade across the road. But it's in vain that I look for crutches, wooden legs and screeching parrots stuffed behind doors or into carved elephant feet.

The comfortably dim lighting accentuates the greyness of the sky scowling angrily through the window. It's difficult in such inclement weather to imagine how in those long-drawn summer evenings the hordes lounge outside to the accompaniment of clanking boats and yachts, taking in the last dregs of the sun as it sets in a blaze of orange somewhere behind Anglesey's bulk.

Across the water lies Moel y Don, scene of a blood-thirsty battle between the Druid-led locals and the Roman invaders all of 2,000 years ago, long before the advent of extra-cold lager became an excuse for such behaviour in some quarters.

The yellow-wellington-boots brigade with their pretend captain's peaked caps that swarm all over the Garddfon in summer are nowhere to be seen this afternoon; it quite obviously isn't the weather for yachtsmen and other amateur Captain Pugwashes to take to even the protected waters of the Strait.

Instead the place hums with laughter and a sense of camaraderie between the largely retired clientele, huddled around tables or balancing precariously on stools by the bar, and the pleasant staff.

It's abuzz with tales of yore being related in Welsh in this corner, in English over there.

The rather gloomier and, on the surface, less welcoming public bar stays eerily silent as it's shunned by all save those passing through on their way to the toilets.

The background music remains exactly there – nicely in the background, with some gargling nonentity or other struggling to make himself heard over the chatter. Or could it possibly be herself?

Halves are supped with gusto in this Robinson's owned hostelry: the brewer's own Old Stockport is the only cask ale on the bar, but lager drinkers are well-catered for with Fosters, Stella, Carling and its extra-cold brother fighting for space on the counter.

However quite a number seem to be here for the food as much as the drink. While the pub boasts its own separate bistro, the lunchtime clientele pick their spots in this two-part lounge – evidently two separate rooms in a previous existence – as they wait patiently for their meals to be placed before them. And all without a timber being shivered.

Garddfon Inn, Beach Road, Y Felinheli LL56 4RQ.
01248 670359
www.frederic-robinson.com

GARTHANGHARAD,
LLWYNGWRIL, NEAR TYWYN

THE lights still twinkle from the windows of the Garthangharad, welcoming the weary traveller much as it would've done in the days of Abram Wood.

The legendary king of the Welsh Romanies, spared the traditional gypsy's pyre and buried just down the road at Llangelynnin churchyard after his death in 1799, would've been pleased.

He had a penchant for southern Meirionnydd between its isolated foothills and the Cardigan Bay coast which drew him back time and again. The roads might be metalled these days, and the streets lit, but little else has changed in reality since his wagon train trundled past.

Standing on a sharp bend in the road within hearing of the rushing waters of the Gwril at Llwyngwril, the modern traveller in his horseless carriage has little choice but to slow down on approaching the Garthangharad. That's no bad thing.

Others stand panting across the road having scrambled up the hill from the village's tiny unmanned railway halt on the Cambrian Coast line, a service on which you have to ask the guard whether he or she would be good enough to request that the driver stops for you.

A patchwork of tiny rooms, they still manage to cram in a restaurant, a bar and a lounge at the Garthangharad, and if you strike lucky you might well hear live music here too. Abram would've liked that, he and his family being leading exponents of Welsh gypsy harp music.

The pub is named after the estate in Dolgellau of the Owen family, minor gentry who owned much property in these parts right until the early 20th century.

The bar on your right as you enter resembles a cosy waiting

room, the more adventurous squeezing onto the bench in the tiny disused inglenook fireplace.

Visitors – or possibly even new residents to these parts – warily peep over their menus on hearing spoken Welsh. Convinced for some reason that they're the main topic of conversation, they shuffle uncomfortably in their underwear, sinking ever lower in their seats as if trying to trigger some automatic translation device.

Meanwhile the hum of voices drifting over through the compact serving area indicates that a number of locals have settled in the lounge to put the world to rights. The names of the odd politician occasionally surface, laced with colourful adjectives and expletives, only to be shunted aside by more meaningful ones of footballing millionaires.

The energetic barman handles the whole affair with great aplomb. He's head barman, takes orders for food, and doubles as the wine waiter as he hands out bottles of French table wine magically transformed into house wines with the application of home-made sticky labels. All admirably very Blue Peterish.

He proceeds to shepherd another couple through to the restaurant. Abram Wood and his tribe would've appreciated his efforts. The harps no doubt would've been playing well into the night.

Garthangharad, Llwyngwril
LL37 2UZ.
01341 250484

GAZELLE HOTEL,
GLYNGARTH

TIME was, in the 19th century, when people would gather at the Gazelle Tavern on the banks of the Menai Strait to await their ferry from Anglesey to the mainland.

With the pier across the water in Bangor seemingly tantalisingly within reach, little wonder that the Borough of Bangor purchased the pub and surrounding land for this express purpose, seeking to promote the ferry crossing as an alternative to Telford's newfangled Menai Suspension Bridge.

Nowadays people gather here more for reason of relaxation than transportation, the Gazelle lounging in a sun-trap that's as exquisite as any you're likely to find anywhere in Europe.

It's no surprise that the Glyngarth area it stands in, just outside Menai Bridge, has long been dubbed Millionaires' Row, even boasting the odd private islet linked by causeways to Anglesey proper.

House prices have long since soared into the stratosphere, and it's easy to understand why. Given improved weather on a regular basis, the area could easily compete with the French Riviera.

With the pub blessed by stunning views stretching from the Great Orme in one direction, extending over Penrhyn Castle, the majesty of Snowdonia and the tree-lined avenues of Bangor's posher parts across the water, to Telford's bridge in the other direction, the vista has the beating of cinemascope or high-definition telly any day.

One understands why the millionaires descended here when a million quid really was a fortune.

Tipplers enjoy a drink or a meal on the picnic tables right above the Strait's lapping waters at the bottom of the excruciatingly narrow lane that plunges down to the pub's car park. The chatter is distinctly low key, the clatter of plates being scraped clean and the splashing of the water over the stone slipway drowning out most of the chit-chat.

A youngster breaks the trance as he chucks boulders off the narrow, rocky beach into the wavelets, unhindered by any parental chastening.

Meanwhile a couple of men struggle to bring in their rubber dinghy from their boat moored some 100 yards offshore, the strong current mocking their best efforts. Not really caring for the audience they've garnered, they grin sheepishly.

Inside this Robinson's pub a collection of small snug-type rooms awaits.

They include one complete with brick-fronted fireplace that any grandmother would've been pleased to use as the best parlour for offering the vicar or minister tea and *bara brith*.

They're all however light and airy, in spite of the low ceilings, saturated in bountiful maritime atmosphere.

Noted for its food and the culinary experience in general, especially if you can secure a seat by the windows in the restaurant, look out for the Gazelle's specials board. It could well include delicacies such as a smoked mackerel salad or a rack of ribs.

Gazelle Hotel, Glyngarth, Menai Bridge LL59 5PD.
01248 713364
www.frederic-robinson.com

GEORGE III HOTEL,
PENMAENPOOL

THE first inkling of a sunny day sees shirts discarded and a clamour for *al fresco* dining and drinking. Perhaps it's why Swansea poet Kathryn Gray, among others, wrote about her fellow Welsh as "Italians in the rain".

So sitting in a concreted back yard or on a fume-infested pavement might not be what you had in mind, but what the heck?

However Wales is generously endowed with bars and hotels offering pristine environments and genuinely stunning vistas from the table where you've plonked your pint. And there can be few to equal the peace and beauty that surrounds you at the George III Hotel in Penmaenpool.

With the wide expanses of the Mawddach lumbering lazily past the front door on its way to the sea at Barmouth, it's not difficult to imagine the time when the quayside on which the hotel stands bristled with ships.

Penmaenpool was once a boom port famous for its boat building industry, and indeed one half of the hotel used to be a ship chandler's workshop. It's quiet on the river these days, although the odd fishing boat or pleasure craft still ties up.

The quayside is separated from the hotel by the bed of the former Cambrian Railway, callously axed by Beeching in 1964, and the lodge which forms part of the hotel's accommodation was once a waiting room, ticket office and station master's house.

One of the now defunct signals still stands to attention by the track-bed, waiting in hope for the mournful whistle of one last train that might approach from Dolgellau.

Inside it's a rambling warren of bars and rooms over two floors, most of it proudly showing off its great age, the building reckoned to have stood here since about 1650. It still sighs with understandable pleasure on waking up to the sights that surround it each morning.

Look for the intriguing bar counter upstairs created out of an old dresser, and the grotto-like snug around the corner where comfy armchairs gather like lazy cats around an open fire for when the chill sets in as the orange sun surrenders to nightfall.

It has reaped quite a reputation for itself as a place to enjoy a bar meal while taking in the view. The menu typically offers pub staples such as steak and ale pie, chilli con carne with rice, or quiche with salad, although it's revamped on a regular basis.

But the George's *piece de resistance* can be best described in just three words: location, location, location. Order a pint of your favourite ale and sit by one of the tables outside, particularly the one teetering dizzily right on the quayside edge if you can grab it.

With the rumbling of the occasional vehicle rolling gently across the wooden toll bridge nearby lulling you to dreamland, sit back and enjoy a rare tranquil treat.

George III Hotel, Penmaenpool LL40 1YD.
01341 422525
www.georgethethird.co.uk

GLAN YR AFON INN,
DOLPHIN

"CONSERVATIVES", the lady sitting by the door tells me breezily as I enter the Estuary Bar just off the metal footbridge crossing from the car park. It's neither question nor statement, really, just an utterance.

I've been accused of many things in my time, but being a Tory is a new one. Not really looking for an eighth sin to boast about, finding seven more than enough to juggle with, I hastily retreat and retrace my footsteps.

A spluttering of smokers gathered in a carcinogenic cloud around a picnic table indicates where the front door to this intriguing 16th century inn lies. They pay little heed to the majestic splendour of the vista laid out down the hillside in front of them, with the sun setting in orange glory over the Dee in England's smog.

The chimneys of the chemical plants across the water gleefully join in the pollution game, chuckling rudely as they spew their poisons into the evening sky. Yet even that fails to mar the magic of the glorious ginger sunset that has the estuary in its breathtakingly hypnotic grasp.

I comfort myself with the thought that the Glan yr Afon boasts a host of *al fresco* options that simply cries out for a bit of cuddly global warming.

They include an useful children's play area, complete with grinning plastic tree-trunk, that's cleverly set out by the car park away from the rest of the gardens and out of adult earshot.

The pub actually stands above the Milwr Tunnel, a 10-mile long drainage tunnel excavated to lower the water table and allow the lead mines peppering Halkyn Mountain nearby to work to even greater depths.

Should you fancy having a peek at the workings, have a word

with the enthusiasts from the Grosvenor Caving Club who use the pub as their base.

This place is a rabbit warren of bars propped up by broad beams, and I make my way past a forest of candle-lit tables to a slice of counter near an unseasonal open fire to check out on their liquid wares.

The place prides itself on supporting micro-brewers, and you might even find the Porthmadog-based Purple Moose Brewery having made inroads all the way eastwards here into Flintshire.

Hardly had I sat down on a settle by a farmhouse-type table than a waiter asked if I was ready to order. And there was I thinking I already had.

This is as much a restaurant as it is a pub, as one would expect in a tiny hamlet such as the intriguingly-named Dolphin, just up the road from Holywell.

The menu is huge and varied, and amongst the chalked-up treats tonight are lamb shank and rainbow trout. Salivating intensely, I decide nonetheless that tonight's not the night for solo dining, if there ever is such an occasion, and stick with Purple Moose's finest.

Glan yr Afon Inn, Dolphin, Holywell CH8 8HE.
01352 710052
www.glanyrafoninn.co.uk

GLYN VALLEY HOTEL,
GLYN CEIRIOG

"JUST passing through, are you?" barks Stuart – if I've eavesdropped his name correctly – as a wave of suspicion sweeps over his bar at the Glyn Valley Hotel.

As welcomes go, it could just about be beaten. I wonder if writer George Borrow had the same problem when he supped here in 1854 as he researched his classic *Wild Wales* travelogue.

I wouldn't mind, but it's not as if you actually pass through Glyn Ceiriog to get anywhere in particular. Not without traversing mountain roads best left to 4x4 vehicles.

The clientele propping up the bar chortles politely at Stuart's wit. I ponder whether it's my accent – being distinctly different to the Shropshire burr many have adopted here almost right on the English border – or my enquiry about what real ales they had that set off Stuart's side-splitting repartee.

It's not that I'm a real ale drinker. I have no intention of investing in sandals nor Fair Isle sweaters, nor of sprouting a great big hairy beard.

It's just that the attention an establishment pays to its rather more troublesome real ales is often an indication of how seriously it takes its reputation. Is it a pub, or a plastic lager lounge?

Locals will tell you that the tinkling brook which dances its way past this stone built inn's foundations keeps the cellar at the optimum temperature for beer. They only have draught Bass on tap this evening, but it's quaffable enough on a stiflingly hot summer evening.

The Glyn Valley seems to be the epicentre of the village's social life. The choir calls in on practice nights, and the local football team uses the place as its clubhouse. A poster in Welsh urges the villagers to support their team in the rather grandly titled Welsh National League – effectively the Wrexham and district league –

rather than any of those fancy-dan outfits across the border.

I pop with pint in hand into a cosy side room near the main bar to witness a fascinating exhibition of photographs and memorabilia of the long-defunct Glyn Valley Tramway. And all for free.

The tramway carried slate from the quarries around here to the mainline Great Western Railway at Chirk until 1935. Its supporters have hopes of some day restoring part of the line, but in the meantime this is the Tramway Group's official museum.

The hotel is in fact a rabbit warren of bars and function rooms. A cavernous games room *en route* to the toilets, with two huge one-armed bandits winking at you suggestively in the corner, is very much a 1970s throwback. In fact the whole hotel is tinged in comforting sepia, as if time had stood still almost since when Borrow called.

As I venture to the picnic tables outside to take in lurid tales of the day's shopping trips to Oswestry, I wonder if they'd changed much since Borrow's time. He'd have been disappointed if they had.

Glyn Valley Hotel, Glyn Ceiriog, near Chirk LL20 7EU.
01691 718896
www.glynvalley.co.uk

GOLDEN FLEECE,
TREMADOG

THERE are few squares anywhere that match the majesty of that in Tremadog, a fine early example of a planned town that never quite grew to the proportions envisaged by its wealthy creator William Madocks.

That a small village such as this should boast its own Town Hall with its own quintet of arches as a façade – now a fashion shop – seems quite preposterous. It's just one of a number of impressive stone buildings that form the perimeter of the square, lying in the shadow of the sheer cliff face hovering menacingly above.

Three of them, to the delight of the weary traveller passing this way on the tortuous A487, or just the committed pub crawler, are public houses-cum-eateries. Another is a restaurant of some reputation.

The Golden Fleece is an inn that has long been a favourite among locals and those just passing through, a famous old coaching house that reeks of history and atmosphere as I push open the front door.

Turning to the left, I pass an intriguing head-height wooden partition behind which I hear female giggling and the clinking of plates, an early evening meal evidently forming the basis of an opportunity to catch up on local chit-chat. If not even downright scandals.

Sadly, I can't quite catch what's being said in this snuggest of snugs, which uses an open door to the servery area as a means of getting its drinks. Meanwhile the bar proper is known as the Cave Bar.

The reason for this soon becomes clear as mine host expertly makes his way around the arched one-time wine cellar that's his domain without once banging his head as he pulls his pints.

The real ale offering is interesting enough, tonight featuring the local Purple Moose Brewery's Snowdonia Ale and that old favourite, Draught Bass, amongst others.

I wimpishly opt for a fruit juice, drawing some strange looks from a man at the bar who's excitedly explaining about some brush with officialdom in very industrial language with another patron. The latter eventually makes his escape as his meal turns up.

Two other men grin sagely, nursing their pints like hot mugs of tea, as they sit in comfortable armchairs either side of a blazingly hot fire.

This black-beamed room is quaintly old fashioned, with many of the bench seats sagging contentedly as they think of the thousands of back-sides they've uncomplainingly accommodated down the years.

Every Tuesday night folk music aficionados make their way here for a jamming session that's long been part of the weekly entertainment in these parts.

The bar menu features pub favourites such as chicken Kiev or scampi, while the Little Ivy restaurant in the old stable block across the cosy and fully-covered courtyard features a more extensive menu.

Golden Fleece Inn, Tremadog LL49 9RB.
01766 512421
www.goldenfleeceinn.com

GOLDEN LION,
WREXHAM

THE gust blowing through the glass-covered alleyway between the Golden Lion and its JD Wetherspoon neighbour, one of the new breed of super-pubs ensconced in a former bank, would've had Bruce Forsyth clasping his hair piece in horror.

An ideal extended drinking space offering the *al fresco* experience on its picnic tables coupled with shelter from the worst vagaries of the Welsh weather, one would've imagined it provided the ideal smokers' refuge.

Not a bit of it. Their designated area is shunted up right at the far end, beyond civilisation and past where the glass veranda judders to an end, where they shiver beneath a parasol warming their hands around their Embassy Regals.

The Golden Lion is a long streak of ancient history extending into near eternity through four separate yet interlinked areas, the wooden floor merging into stone before emerging as wood again where lunchtime revellers are enjoying a game of pool right at the back.

Originally the home of the Pulford family, this Grade II listed building was an iconic one in medieval Wrexham. Built in the 17th century, it was first licensed as a public house in 1684. Later used as shops, it had reverted to its use as an inn by 1740.

Tidied up more than modernised, it has thankfully escaped the scourge of modern pub designers and their penchant for plastic Victoriana, while remaining a popular music venue for the younger generation who throng to this part of town at weekends.

Its status as a younger people's pub is amply underlined by its choice between glistening chilled fonts of Stella Artois, Fosters and Budweiser lagers on the bar.

Strangely, though, the speakers on the wall remain mute throughout my visit, the place simply humming of its own antiquity rather than reverberating to the thud-thud beat typical of Radio 1 that must pervade the place after dark.

The front part of the building reveals some of the original timber frame on the gable end. This part is given over largely to dining at certain times of the day, taking on larger neighbour next door with a competitively priced menu that might offer fish and chips, chicken kiev or a mixed grill.

A group of pleasant young diners chat contentedly in an accent that is part Scouse and part south Wales valleys through full mouths, alternating between chomping chips and supping draughts of insipid Bud; the American copy rather than the much more fulfilling Czech original.

They get up and leave as 2pm approaches, the clock forcing them ruefully back to their offices before they're able to clear their plates.

Then a cool silence descends on the place, broken only by the clicking of pool balls and the clinking of a gaming machine as it gleefully accepts its bearded adherent's tokens of gratitude.

Golden Lion Inn, High Street, Wrexham LL13 8HP.
01978 340051

HARP INN,
ABERGELE

THE young woman's hair is almost as red as the bottleful of alcopop she grasps as she seeks somewhere to sit that's to her liking. It's early evening, and perhaps a bit too early for many of her tender years to be out painting the town the same hue, but the rest of the clientele is a bit more mature in years. Yes, yes, including yours truly.

And although the piped music is somewhat obtrusive, with speakers wired up everywhere ensuring you can hear it everywhere from the foyer even right into the toilets, it is distinctly middle-of-the-road stuff being pumped out. Old fashioned, even, to the discerning ears of Ms Redhead and her generation weaned on more thumping variations.

She nonetheless finally decides on a table in one of the several corners she could have chosen from, and settles down to a good old chin-wag with a friend about the trials and tribulations of her young life.

Come daytime and Abergele reverts more to its agricultural past, as farmers and country dwellers from the outlying villages come into town for a spot of shopping, interspersed with the odd pint or two.

By night it transforms itself back into its more urban guise, perhaps surprisingly for a town of its size, but probably explained by the increasingly deep thrusts of Merseyside's cultural tentacles along the northern coastal belt.

The groups of people sitting in human dollops here and there certainly seem to be displaying the city dweller's penchant for interacting with their own small circle of acquaintances rather than mixing in with everyone in general, as you tend to find in village pubs. But perhaps the alcohol hasn't kicked in just yet, and the place nonetheless radiates a friendly enough atmosphere.

The Harp Inn is a fascinating old place, reputedly the oldest house in Abergele and once just one of 16 public houses in town that kept the drinking public entertained.

It was also in a previous incarnation a jail, the local lock-up where drunkards and petty criminals were held while awaiting their turn to be put in the stocks to be pelted with what rotting vegetation the populace at large could afford to toss at them. So much more effective than fixed penalty fines or community service.

Today it's a warren of former rooms largely knocked together, although maintaining sufficient partitions and discreet corners to give a semblance at least of allowing some privacy to get on with whatever one feels like doing down at the inn.

A huge inglenook fireplace laid out in a farmhouse kitchen style, complete with ladles, firewood and a huge mangle your gran's neighbours would have gagged for, takes pride of place. The unlit grate nestles lazily in its place in a black-leaded range that in its heyday would've called for half a morning's attention each day. How so uncivilised.

Harp Inn, Market Street, Abergele LL22 7AF.
01745 824080

HOLE IN THE WALL INN,
CAERNARFON

HACKS have traditionally adopted a pub to skulk in at the end of a hectic working day; quite often even during the day when deadlines are at least a relaxing two hours away.

Such was the Hole in the Wall Inn for me many moons ago when I earned my crust, if precious little else save for some beer money, beavering away for the local paper in a cramped office around the corner.

The pub lies right in the lea of the majestic medieval walls surrounding the town proper. The outside loos in those days, a short dash across a rainy back yard, leaned disrespectfully on a major feature of those walls, since been designated part of a World Heritage Site by UNESCO. Who would've thought as we stood there all those years ago?

The place was mercifully little afflicted by the sunlight that makes hangovers that much worse; its cool 1930s interior made for that perfect 11am refuge from the little men with miniature jackhammers working away at my fevered cranium.

How times have changed. Not only does the thought of nursing a hangover seem a touch too masochistic, but the Hole in the Wall too has changed beyond all recognition.

Its two miniature bars have been opened up into one airy - if still compact - space, its colour scheme a bright and breezy combination of terracotta and calf's excreta.

The outside loos are of course no more, but a salvaged pub mirror bearing the legend "Your local" and a photograph of the exterior as it used to look when owned my Marstons brings the memories flooding back.

The narrow pedestrianised street it stands on could for all the world be a pretty German gasse, in summer a colourful and delightful melee of bunting and *al fresco* drinking and dining.

The developers of the pub weren't slow in realising its potential, fitting it with French doors leading out onto the lane in clement weather.

It's delightfully relaxed and quiet this early evening, the odd early doors customer relaxing on its oddments of furniture reading newspapers left out for their use.

Nobody pays any attention to Jasper Carrott jabbering away on a tiny TV set fixed up high in a corner, and the juke-box yawns idly on the wall, waiting for somebody to feed it.

One gentleman is nearly at full stretch on a deeply upholstered sofa as he peruses the *Daily Post*, enjoying his spot of relaxation before heading off for home.

He'll be long gone by the time the karaoke and disco takes over. I recall how a chap with a synthesiser and poor command of Welsh used to be squeezed into a corner here, paid good money to murder traditional folk airs. Happy days. Even with the hangovers.

Hole in the Wall Inn,
Hole in the Wall Street, Caernarfon LL55 1RF.
01286 678464

HORSE AND JOCKEY,
WREXHAM

THE dazzlingly-polished brass fittings through which the golden nectar known as Wrexham Lager flowed by the gallon have long since gone, replaced largely by modern extra-cold cousins with more fizz than flavour.

But the now-defunct company's sign remains by the front door on the corner of Hope Street, sheltering from the chill blast of winter sweeping in off the Llandegla moors beneath those rare thatched eaves that mark out the Horse and Jockey from other town centre pubs.

It's a welcome reminder of how things were, when Wrexham was a booming brewing town with a number of established breweries, now sadly all gone.

Border Brewery, which came up with that clever marketing slogan "The Prince of Ales" and who were the sponsors after whom the Border Stand at Wrexham FC's stadium was named, closed its gates for the last time in 1984. The Wrexham Lager Brewery, established in 1882 by German and Czech immigrants, went the same way in 2000.

The pub is a timber-framed building that's stood here since the 17th century, and is one of the few urban inns in Wales that boasts a thatched roof. It has been used as an inn for at least two centuries, with the present premises emerging from the merger of a private house and a small alehouse known as the Colliers back in 1868.

The establishment would later take its present name in honour of Fred Archer, a local champion jockey who made his name just down the road at Bangor-on-Dee racecourse. He died in 1886, aged just 29.

Many moons have passed since I first popped in here. It's survived fires and attempts at redevelopment, and it's retained its character as a comfortable drinkers' den.

However it's a case of needs must, and it would be foolish of a town centre pub – especially one so full of character – to spurn the opportunity to offer meals and hot drinks. Shoppers huddle over a steaming cappuccino while at the next table young men in denims gulp their alcoholic fizz.

The main bar has an utilitarian slate floor and an unbelievably low-beamed ceiling that reminds one of how short of stature people were when this building was first erected. But the Horse and Jockey has that certain Tardis quality; it's surprisingly larger inside than one would guess before stepping over the threshold into the gleaming warm refuge it offers.

I wander through to the compact dining area only to find it unsurprisingly deserted in late afternoon, with no takers for its all-day breakfast. However gales of laughter flooding out of a side room, in years past the haunt of dominoes players hiding their cards behind nicotine-stained fingers in the flickering gloom, indicates that the bar is still busy enough. Gratified, I leave.

Horse & Jockey, Hope Street, Wrexham LL11 1BD.
01978 351081

KING'S HEAD,
LLANDUDNO

THERE are no whistles nor clouds of steam to indicate that the 14.20 is about to leave the station next door. Just a distant rumble, then a blue shadow eclipsing the light through the bar room window, as another tram trundles off sedately on its mile-long haul to the top of the Great Orme.

This cable-hauled tramway, inaugurated in 1902, is one of Llandudno's best enduring tourist attractions. And it's only fitting that it should sit cheek to jowl with the King's Head, reputedly the oldest pub in Llandudno, snuggled up cosily next to each other on the hillside on Old Road, in what was the original part of town.

It's said that it was over a jug of ale in here in the mid-19th century that the land-owning Mostyn dynasty was first alerted to the then tiny village's huge tourist potential by surveyor Owen Williams. He proposed a massive expansion and the building of plush three- and four-storey hotels along the seaside. The rest, as they say, is history.

It was the steepness of the roads in these parts that sparked off the idea of building the tramway, the Victorian visitors unwilling to contemplate the laborious walk to the summit, especially in their full-length dresses. As for the ladies …

Sitting in the Kings Head as the tram takes the strain today, grunting its way past up the Orme, I imagine the horrific scene that struck the area one Wednesday back in August 1932.

The bar attaching the cable to tram number 4 inexplicably snapped, the tram careering down the hill uncontrollably before crashing into a wall. Two people were killed and several others badly injured.

It's much more sedate here today. The pub is still hugely atmospheric, spared some of the worst excesses of the huge summer influx by being just that bit away from the town centre.

With a sprawling central bar servery as the hub, it offers several distinctive areas on split levels that would in the distant past no doubt have been separate rooms.

Comfortably illuminated by dim lighting that accentuates the gloom of the scowling clouds outside, it has just a few punters seated here and there this mid-afternoon. One couple sit in silent meditation over their halves of lager.

The office workers have flitted back to their desks having taken their fill from the pub's extensive lunchtime menu, which includes tap room favourites such as steak and ale pie or cod and chips.

However a collection of nicotine addicts sitting outside in the sizeable beer garden, with its impressive castellated back wall, would explain the interior's Marie Celeste atmosphere.

An impressively long wine list is chalked up behind the bar, which boasts the usual beers one would expect to find. It also has a host of real ales on offer, including Brains SA, Greene King IPA and Abbots Ale.

King's Head, Old Road, Llandudno LL30 2NB.
01492 877993

LAST INN,
BARMOUTH

STRIDING into the cool serenity of the back bar at the Last Inn from the dazzle of the sun outside, it takes some time for my eyes to adjust to the welcoming darkness.

It's not without reason that customers are advised to watch their heads, the low beams viciously lurking in wait for any towering foreheads not wise enough to heed the warning.

Many are ships' timbers salvaged from vessels long since departed, hardly surprising given the inn's position right on the colourful harbourside in a town with such a rich maritime tradition.

One can almost hear the hushed groanings of ghostly contraband-laden boats being rowed ashore, and it's easy to imagine Jolly Jack Tars puffing on their pipes on the quayside opposite.

Gradually it dawns on me that the place is largely lit by candles flickering on the tables, squeezed higgledy-piggledy wherever this ancient building has decreed should have a suitable nook here or a cranny there.

As I await my turn at the bar while the staff dash about with orders for meals, a gentle tinkling of water threatens to send me into a karma-like trance, even before the alcohol kicks in.

The pub leans on the mountainside behind it, fresh spring water trickling down the open crag-face into a cooling well where colourful carp slumber peacefully. This used to be the pub's cellar in earlier times, where the naturally-chilled water kept casks of ale cool well before the advent of extra-cold lager.

I grasp my pint of artificially-chilled cider and settle down beneath a canopy of dried hops in a corner dedicated to the town's legion of lifeboat crews, who down the years have risked and sometimes lost their lives in the service of others.

This 15th century building is known as the Last Inn, not because of its position on the edge of town, but from its previous name as the Cobbler's Last, once the house where a local shoemaker decided he'd put his feet up in retirement. Or so the story goes.

The place is abuzz with diners, with lunchtime offerings including jacket potatoes and a hearty ploughman's lunch. Meanwhile my lips go into involuntary smacking mode as the specials' board for the evening ahead announces that lamb shank and Chinese roast duck will be on the menu.

The front bar is an altogether lighter and airier affair with a more modern feel, while tourists and locals enjoying their lunch breaks scramble for a seat outside in one of the pew-like arrangements nestling beneath a veranda.

A train trundles at a snail-like pace almost directly overhead as it makes its way towards the famous wooden viaduct crossing the Mawddach, heading slowly but surely to Machynlleth, Aberystwyth and the outside world beyond Shrewsbury. The train driver, however, is not the only one in these parts in no great hurry.

Last Inn,
Church Street,
Barmouth LL42 1EL.
01341 280530

LION HOTEL,
BERRIEW

IN a border country dotted with picture postcard villages, few surpass the beauty of Berriew. A tidy jumble of black-timbered houses and shops, cobbled pavements, and an immaculately maintained church, it just calls out for a couple of pubs to complete its rustic charm.

That call is answered by the Talbot Hotel and its Lion Hotel counterpart the other side of the rushing waters of the river Rhiew, from which the village takes its name, an ancient Anglicisation of the original Aberriw.

Seeking shelter from a monsoon-like summer shower that threatens to swell the Rhiew from a trickle to a roar this murky afternoon, we dive into the Lion for refuge.

A gaggle of men in funereal garb chuckling around the bar indicate that a sad farewell has just been bid to somebody at St Beuno's Church, just yards away. Their voices echo from the huge inglenook fireplace that dominates this compact room.

Meanwhile in the lounge, with the church in full panoramic view through the window, others whisper fond reminiscences of the dear departed over halves of bitter or glasses of dry sherry.

The place hums with rural accents that are probably a mixture of Powys and Shropshire, with just a hint of cider drinkers' burr for good measure. Smocks probably wouldn't look dreadfully out of place.

It's comfortably busy for a mid-week afternoon, so much so that we're surprised to be told that they'll be closing any minute now as the seconds hand clicks relentlessly towards 3pm.

So what happened to the much-vaunted all-day drinking some rabid commentators warned was about to descend on us like the Four Horsemen of the Apocalypse? We could do with some right now.

We grudgingly accept an offer of a drink on condition it's consumed quickly, given it's still teeming outside. We almost feel as if we're intruding, but settle down in the corner nonetheless to hurriedly down our soft drinks.

The Lion is an AA two-star establishment that has a restaurant and bistro in addition to offering bar meals, supplemented today by chalked-up specials.

The bar offers a varied selection of drinks and real ales, which include the 4.1% ABV Hooky Gold and Marston's Old Empire on hand-pull.

The building itself is a maze of rooms that almost circle up on themselves, with exposed beams and original wattle and daub revealing its origins as a 17th century coaching inn. It has managed to retain its medieval charm while imbuing it in 21st century comfort.

Even the toilets are a delight to behold, refreshingly spotless and odourless, with the powder room once having been nominated for the Best Ladies' Loo Award. High praise indeed.

Sufficiently impressed if rather rushed, we step out of the front door onto the cobbled forecourt to find the monsoon easing off. We'll be back, time and weather permitting.

Lion Hotel, Berriew, Powys SY21 8PQ. 01686 640452
www.thelionhotelberriew.co.uk

LIVERPOOL ARMS,
CONWY

IN DAYS past you'd be grateful for the warning etched on the Victorian windows staring out over the quay. Clearly spelling out Smoke Room, rarely can there have been a more honest statement of intent. In marketing parlance, you'd clearly get what it says on the tin.

You'd grope your way through a heavy nicotine-laden smog worthy of any Jack the Ripper movie to get to the bar, occasionally tripping over a languid dog lying flat out on the floor. Obviously suffering from nicotine poisoning.

Times, however, change. The air these days is so clear you can virtually taste the brine in it.

Some say that the Liverpool Arms was thus named because it was a waiting room for passengers embarking on the ferries to and from the city.

It won't have changed much over the decades, although the fare-charging boats anchored directly opposite nowadays take their passengers no further than up and down Afon Conwy's powerful sweep.

Just yards away stands the famous smallest house in Britain, a tiny sliver of terrace outside of which a lady in national costume often stands to whip up trade.

A single-roomed L-shaped inn bursting at the seams with character, the Liverpool Arms has somehow managed to incorporate itself into the medieval town walls built by Edward I to keep the wicked Welsh out. Natural light struggles to make any headway past the heavily-curtained windows, imparting a cosy winter's afternoon atmosphere to the place even in mid-summer.

A garrulous wedding party, one of them resplendent in a natty if adventurous kilt, adds to the noisy melee as it awaits orders to make its way elsewhere.

This is clearly a drinker's pub, and none the worse for it, with men and women equally at ease here. Any request for food triggers the barmaid's finger, pointing out the filled baps whimpering in expectation on a plate awaiting new owners.

It's blessed with an idyllic location almost within smelling distance of the famed mussel beds, overlooking the posh houses across the river on Deganwy's marina that few around here could afford.

It's one of Wales' finest locations to while away a few hours over the odd pint, although on fine days *al fresco* drinkers must tolerate dive-bombing seagulls chasing soggy chips tossed to them by the brainless. Don't they understand the theories of digestion, which rules that what goes in must come out? Usually with a splatter.

However it's not much of a problem today, being a typical Welsh summer's day. With the rain coming down in stair-rods, Mancunian and Liverpudlian holiday-makers stoically don their wellies and their sou'westers to make the best of their traditional break beneath the parasols on the picnic tables outside.

Meanwhile the jackdaws, as residents of Conwy are nicknamed, although in reality it refers to those born within the town walls, prefer the comfort of the bar with its instant access to service. I'm with them on that one.

Liverpool Arms,
Lower Gate Street,
Conwy LL32 8BE.
01492 596464

LLEW COCH,
DINAS MAWDDWY

IT'S said that the four requisites of a living, breathing village are a place of worship, a pub, a school and a shop.

While Dinas Mawddwy sadly lacks the latter, it has the remainder. Indeed it boasts three pubs within its perimeters, notwithstanding parochial squabbles about where Dinas ends and the neighbouring hamlet of Minllyn begins.

Probably the better known of that triumvirate of good living is the ancient inn known variously as the Llew Coch or the Red Lion according to which side of the linguistic fence one falls.

Dating back to the 12th century, one can almost hear its ancient stone walls whispering tales of philandering, jollity, plotting and good old fashioned raucousness stretching back into the mists of time. Not that things have changed much. The old place remains an important social hub as much as a popular watering hole for travellers on this main north-south artery, as it's always been.

It was its strategic position on this pass through the mountains that made the locality an ideal spot for a touch of banditry and highway robbery in the 15th and 16th century. Travellers were plagued by Gwylliaid Cochion Mawddwy, the famed red haired bandits. Baron Lewis Owen, the spoilsport that he was, put a spoke in their activities in 1554 when he had many of them hanged.

Although the Brigands' Inn up the road in Mallwyd is reputed to have been one of their meeting places, they'd doubtless also have swaggered into the Llew Coch to swap tales of the day's murder and mayhem. You can almost hear them chortling into their pre-1554 beer mugs.

The language of the place has changed much in recent years in the wake of the huge influx from across the border, and you're almost as likely to hear a Brummie accent as a native one on some nights. But the ruddy-faced locals born and bred here still stand out, chatting away in their Montgomeryshire-tinged Welsh – although the village has been under Meirionnydd's jurisdiction for centuries.

Stroll into the compact public bar with its imposing inglenook fireplace and you'll be dazzled by an array of brassware. One suspects that a tanker full of Brasso must pull up outside every other week.

The huge battered table that takes centre stage must have had millions of pint pots plonked on its gnarled surface, and many a colourful night is still spent gathered around it. Another table in the corner is known among many of the locals as the "bwrdd meddwi" – the "tipplers' table" from which you're unlikely to leave the premises in a state approaching anything like sobriety.

Across the corridor stands a games room, while down the bottom of a sloping corridor you'll find a cavernous family room used for dining, receptions or entertainment, the inn still being a bit of a musical hot spot should you hit the right night.

Red Lion, Dinas Mawddwy SY20 9JA.
01650 531247
www.llewcoch.co.uk

LLINDIR INN,
HENLLAN

THERE'S just something about thatched pubs that draws the curious into their welcoming bosom.

It's that certain fairy tale magnetism that attracts one to its door, just as surely as Little Red Riding Hood would've found herself making her way jauntily into her gran's house even as the wicked wolf audibly licked his lips in greedy anticipation.

The Llindir Inn falls into that category. The Brothers Grimm wouldn't be out of place if they were quilling a sequel at the table squeezed almost into the inglenook fireplace over there in the corner.

The flames' comforting red glow twinkles off the plethora of brass pinned on the wooden lintel above.

One of the Frederic Robinson estate of inns, this 13th century building is believed to be one of the oldest in Wales to still have its thatch intact. Little wonder the walls whisper at me to listen to their tales as I make my way in.

Locals will tell you the place is indeed haunted, as I'd suspect of any self-respecting hostelry of this vintage.

They murmur that she's an attractive young woman all dressed in white. What else? Bored by her mariner husband's globe-trotting, she acquired a lover, but was murdered by her spouse when he returned home unexpectedly and caught them in an act of adultery.

What happened to her lover goes unrecorded. He's probably still shivering in fear for his life in some secret closet.

The Llindir is named after the flax (*llin* in Welsh) which was once a mainstay crop in these parts. It stands opposite the ancient church of St Sadwrn and its quirky detached tower, perched on a rocky outcrop so that the bells could be heard further away than if they were sited in the church proper.

The pub is split into a Top Bar, furnished with luxurious leather furniture to lounge in like a contented moggie, and a slightly more utilitarian Bottom Bar. They're separated by just three steps, too short to merit being labelled a flight.

Then there's the TV lounge for the soap addicts, and the games room with darts and pool for those into just that shade more exercise than merely propping up the bar.

Of course the food offering is an essential aspect of most pub operations these days, and the Llindir is no exception.

In addition to the bars, it also offers the option of a comfortable 50-cover restaurant. The bilingual menu has a range of meals to suit most appetites, from the petite to the positively ravenous.

Lunchtime sees options such as a smoked salmon sandwich, ploughman's salad or that traditional pub staple, gammon and chips, served with the ubiquitous fried egg or pineapple slice.

Meanwhile in the evenings it expands to include favourites such as Welsh lamb shank or a juicy ribeye steak, while the specials board is always worth keeping an eye on.

Llindir Inn, Henllan, near Denbigh LL16 5BH.
01745 815112
www.llindirinn.com

NEW INN,
LLANRWST

NOT having ventured over the threshold of the New Inn since the National Eisteddfod hit town one wild week back in 1989, but having been told it's been newly refurbished, it's with a mixture of excitement and trepidation that I push open the door.

After all, doesn't refurbishment usually equate to character and tradition being ripped out, to be replaced by plastic tat, screwed-on black beams and make-believe Victoriana? Not that I'd have taken in the décor during Eisteddfod week in the first place.

I needn't have worried. If indeed the New Inn has been under the refurbisher's hammer and saw, it certainly doesn't stand out for the uninitiated. With the shoppers on the street outside dashing about like fury looking for those last minute bargains, it presents a welcoming haven from the shopping mania.

The first thing that strikes you on walking in is the gleaming wooden floor that seems to go on into eternity, or at least as far as the huge inglenook fireplace that huddles behind the pool table at the far end. Its proximity to the pool players' tender regions as they cue up probably lies behind its dormant state.

But worry not, a little snug by the front door at the other end of the pub is illuminated by the heart-warming orangey glow of a roaring fire. The huge dog spread-eagled contentedly in front of it, taking up most of the snug's floor space, evidently loves it too.

Remembering that old adage about what to do about sleeping dogs, and bereft of any alcohol-induced bravery, I decide to redirect my steps to the equally comfortable bar area.

The clientele, apart from a couple of characters sullenly and silently enjoying each other's company wedged against the bar, appears to be largely retired.

One chap in a Sherlock Holmes deerstalker asks another without any fancy dress headgear if he's in town to pick up his pension. And presumably spending as much of it as he can before handing over the residue to the missus.

The brushing drumbeat of the Coronation Street theme bizarrely wafts over from the gloom somewhere between here and the pool table, and I half expect to see a leopard-skin attired Bet Lynch flashing her baubles behind the bar.

I awake from the nightmare just before Ken Barlow walks in for a barney with Mike Baldwin. Then I realise it's a one-armed bandit making the wailing Corrie noises, complete with brushing drumbeat.

The real ale aficionados are certainly spoilt for choice in this Marstons pub. Albert Tatlock would've been impressed, able to choose between Banks' Original, Marstons' own, and the intriguingly named Jennings' Sneck Lifter.

I almost ask the young lady behind the bar what it means, but decide against it in case it should be blindingly obvious. It probably is to anybody from Cockermouth in Cumbria, where it is brewed. And at 5.1% ABV, it probably doesn't matter much once you've had a pint or three.

New Inn,
Denbigh Street,
Llanrwst LL26 0LL.
01492 640476

PENYGWRYD HOTEL,
NANT GWYNANT

ABOUT as Welsh as a pith helmet, the Penygwryd rattles to accents that are more Buckinghamshire than Bangor or Bagillt or Bersham, let alone Bala.

It stands haughtily like some colonial embassy right in the heart of Snowdonia's splendour, wide yellow moors sweeping towards Capel Curig in one direction and the mist-shrouded peak of Snowdon itself dominating the skyline in the other.

As I step inside I can almost imagine the clientele discussing their catch of tigers over a pink gin at the end of a day's hunting, resting their blunderbusses by the crackling fire.

It's been in landlady Jane Pullee's family since 1947, and it certainly feels like a throwback to those days, magnificently preserved in sepia-tinted aspic. It's not without reason that the first repast of the day here, even given its thoroughly Welsh windswept setting, is called an "English breakfast".

I ponder on what sets it out from its Welsh counterpart as I await my turn behind some rather indecisive dreadlocked young mountaineers at the compact bar servery that greets me. Tripe, or elephant ear soup, perhaps? But perhaps not, somehow.

The fact it's served at 8.50am precisely, not 8.45 and absolutely not 8.55, is indicative of the austere quirkiness of this old inn. It has served as base camp for hordes of walkers, scramblers, hikers and climbers that have swarmed to this part of Wales ever since Victorian times.

Then there's the traditional five course dinner, served to the clanging of a gong at 7.30pm on the dot. Woe betide you if you're late: you'd have to seek out a take-away somewhere. They'd do the speaking clock proud.

It was here that the team preparing for the ultimately first successful ascent of Everest – by Westerners, at any rate – stayed as they trained up in the mountains back in 1953.

Look for their signatures on the ceiling of the bar to your left, where today's young pretenders are earnestly discussing "the Mont Blanc circuit", whatever that might be.

At least they're not on about "Cloggie", as the sheer cliff-face nearby is called by the climbing fraternity, insistent on mangling its proper and beautifully descriptive name of Clogwyn Du'r Arddu. That means the Black Cliff of Darkness. Cloggie? Huh!

The Penygwryd, understandably, is packed with mountaineering paraphernalia. The building further reflects on its ingrained austerity: all wooden and stone-flagged floors, plain wooden tables and chairs, and the odd chapel pew. A Methodist preacher might feel at home here.

The bar area itself, the other side of the servery, looks like a baronial hall that could be straight out of a Basil Rathbone film set.

And there's absolutely no music whatsoever, neither piped nor paid for through any new-fangled contraption such as a juke-box. A persistent trilling indicates that the telephone has somehow made its way, though.

The Penygwryd is thankfully very different to the plastic-cloned pubs that often masquerade as watering holes these days.

Pen y Gwryd Hotel, Nant Gwynant LL55 4NT.
01286 870211
www.pyg.co.uk

PLAS COCH HOTEL,
BALA

THE whiff of lunch still hangs tantalisingly in the air, a sure sign of bustle just minutes ago, although the place is now as deserted as the *Marie Celeste.* My footsteps echo across the well-trodden wooden floor to the bar, behind which a pleasant young lady soon makes an appearance.

She concurs that they had just been quite busy, but that everybody had since scampered back to work. She hands me the drivers' curse, a soft drink, and plonks a bell in the shape of a traditional Welsh lady in front of me, telling me in her distinctive Bala Welsh to tinkle it should I require any further attention.

The Plas Coch is a former coaching inn built in about 1780, and has long held a special place in the town's social whirl. It remains a firm favourite on the weekend pub circuit, when revellers traipse the high street from one establishment to another in pursuit of merriment.

With its lurid red painted walls reflecting on its name, Plas Coch translating as the red mansion, it simply demands to be given the requisite attention. It's as much a part of the high street as the green-tinged statue of radical Liberal MP Tom Ellis across the road, who died of typhoid while visiting Egypt in 1899.

I sit down in the enjoyable mid-afternoon silence to people-watch through the window, the high street bustling with locals going about their business like bees around a hive. They've obviously more important things to do than sitting in a pub. I should feel guilty about my privileged position, but the emotion strangely evades me.

Picking up a menu, I see that the usual pub fare is on offer, with local produce being used wherever possible. The specials board spices up the offering with treats such as trout and chips, an unusual but interesting combination, or beef rogan josh.

Plas Coch is just as much a community pub as it is a hotel offering *en-suite* accommodation. The walls are dotted with pictures of Bala's colourful past, and a fascinating 19th century advert for the long-since defunct Welsh Whisky Distillery which survived briefly just up the road in Fron-goch, its demise hastened as much by the inferior quality of its product as by the distillers' scourge of hardline Bible-bashing.

A figurine of comedy legends Laurel and Hardy intoxicatingly leaning against each other grins at you from the mantelpiece above the fireplace.

Entertainment is regularly held in the extensive lounge area, probably several rooms knocked into one sometime in the foggy past. Meanwhile the public bar – served by its own separate front door into the street – is the place to be to keep up with local gossip.

Plas Coch is also obviously a favourite haunt for members of the local rugby fraternity; mounted on the lounge wall are Welsh representative shirts won by local players against those giants of the oval ball game, Sri Lanka and Germany!

Plas Coch Hotel, High Street, Bala LL23 7AB.
01678 520309
www.plascoch.com

QUEEN'S HEAD,
BRYN DU

IT'S been a good few years since I ventured over the threshold of the Queen's Head, when Mrs Evans served her ale straight from the barrel and anybody silly enough to order a lager would find a warm bottle of it plonked straight in their hand.

Any unwelcome visitors would find themselves redirected up the road with the riposte: "There's a good night on in the Maelog tonight".

So it's with fond memories, and a good deal of apprehension that the place might be all plastic tat by now, that I press the latch and push open the heavy door. I needn't have worried.

Sure, it's served by newfangled gas-driven founts these days, with warm beer boasting bits of God-knows-what floating in it just a distant memory. But the rest of this centuries old inn is just what a serviceman returning from the trenches in 1918 might have expected his local to be like.

The snug to your right as you enter is a throw-back to your grandmother's parlour, where the well-upholstered seats would be reserved for the priesthood and other VIP visitors, and only lacks a ticking grandfather clock to make the scene complete. Served by a sliver of a hatch barely wide enough to thrust a farmer's arm through, many's the bit of local gossip that must have been dispensed here.

The partition has been removed from the corridor that used to lead to the back, creating a welcoming open bar area with gleamingly clean stone-flagged floor and a typical farmhouse fireplace. This is where the weekly quiz takes place, and where local sports aficionados watch their favourite teams on the TV in the corner.

Yet another hatch opens from the same serving area, one of three serving hatches in all, the third allowing the younger generation that spend their time playing pool in the games room to get their fill.

The talkative landlady apologises for having a restricted choice of soft drinks. Evidently the locals in these parts have neither time nor need for namby-pamby pop.

She explains that they don't get that many strangers in, the place being just that bit off the beaten track, although in reality little more than a few beach ball's throws inland from the popular tourist resort of Rhosneigr on Anglesey's spectacular north-western coast. The Queen's Head remains very much a local's local at its best. Typical of hostelries that once used to pepper rural Wales, it would be a crying shame if those that most loudly call for their retention fail to offer it support in the most practical way possible. Through the till.

Queen's Head, Bryn Du, Llanfaelog, Anglesey LL63 5RW.
01407 810806

QUEENS HOTEL,
BLAENAU FFESTINIOG

WHILE it has its detractors and more than its fair share of problems, Blaenau Ffestiniog also has a certain alluring quality imbued in those blue-grey slate heaps that almost tumble down to its streets. Not least its affable natives.

With the mountains seemingly ganging up on it, it has the appearance of some of the towns off the tourist trail that pepper the Tatra mountains in Slovakia.

The vista through the grandly-valanced windows in the bar of the Queens Hotel towards the famed Crimea Pass is spectacular indeed, increasingly so since nicotine buffs were banished from the bar.

Rarely, outside of eastern Europe, have I encountered such a high proportion of clientele in a bar indulging in slow mass suicide, joyfully puffing away on their cigarettes, as I did here on a previous visit.

Also visible through the windows in the square outside are the slate fountain presented by the Chamber of Trade in 1983, and a locomotive from the Gloddfa Ganol slate mine, all reminders of the industry that created this town.

The thickly carpeted bar visually resembles a hotel foyer, and one can imagine Noel Coward lounging over a tipple by one of the tables. With cigarette dangling limply from his fingers in those days, of course, albeit probably crammed into a silver holder.

The clientele is a mixture of young and not-so-young, all seemingly getting on fine with one another over the din of the juke-box.

One middle aged man struggles to hear what's being said at the other end of that modern scourge of social drinking, the mobile phone. If only the same was true at this end, as he decides to take the juke-box on and return the compliment with a very audible contribution to the discourse, letting all and sundry know about the trials and tribulations of life back home.

Suddenly he's left shame faced as the room descends into comparative silence, the juke-box suddenly deciding it wants to be fed again. Did he really mean to let us all know all that personal information, some of it best left between himself and his solicitor? Shrink, even.

The bar leads straight on to a very neat looking restaurant, with meals served daily, although it's deserted as I sip my pint by the bar. If you can't wait, then they might well be able to rustle up a bacon or sausage bap.

The bar bristles with the usual offerings from Carlsberg and Carling to Guinness and its extra-cold cousin. However I've opted for fizzy apple concentrate that otherwise goes by the name of draught cider.

Taking in the fresh mountain air on stepping out of the front door, the woman in the bus shelter across the road clings tightly to her hand-bag as she struggles to light up in the breeze that whistles chillingly through the Crimea Pass and ripples her stockings. Smoking ban or no smoking ban, it makes no difference to her.

Queens Hotel, High Street, Blaenau Ffestiniog LL41 3ES.
01766 830055
www.queens-snowdonia.co.uk

RAILWAY INN,
LLANGEFNI

VISIONS of Basil Rathbone, resplendent in natty deer-stalker, chasing vicious baddies along swaying train corridors spring to mind on stepping through the front door. Or could it be mousy Miss Marple?

The Railway Inn is a pub that deserves to be viewed through sulphur-stained sepia-tinted glasses. Standing directly opposite the site of Llangefni's former railway station on the Gaerwen-Amlwch branch line, senselessly shut to passengers by Dr Beeching in 1964 and to freight traffic by 1993, the place tries valiantly to keep up to its name.

And with the rusty track still in place, even if strangled by weeds and red tape, local enthusiasts still dream of seeing the line re-opened some day.

Much of the pub's interior consists of dark wood panelling reminiscent of musty train carriages of old, illuminated by the diagonally aligned British Rail lamp-shades of the period. A garbled announcement on a tinny tannoy about missed connections to Red Wharf Bay wouldn't go amiss.

Yes, there even used to be a sub-branch line to that coastal retreat jutting off from this branch line – and that within living memory.

Metal name-plates on the walls transport one to Conwy and stations beyond, while the theme is maintained but not overdone with pictures of gleaming steam locomotives. Your typical railway anorak would doubtless be in fits of ecstasy.

But the *piece de resistance*, even if probably unintentional, is the cavernous crag on which the whole building leans and which doubles up as a huge windowless gable-end which caps the furthest end of the bar in virtual velvet-like darkness.

In years past surface water used to flow down the crag face

through the pub and out of the front door.

Nowadays they're better organised, with a soak-away drain guzzling up any excess water and the crag face dry enough to hang a widescreen TV on.

The largely male clientele seems to be taking only a passing interest in a football match being broadcast, but one or two hoot excitedly as some team or other scores.

The Railway is a JW Lees pub, a family-owned Manchester brewery which maintains an estate of some 30 outlets in northern Wales.

It offers the company's own in-house cask ale, which seems to be popular enough amongst the locals, but precious few namby-pamby soft drinks for those such as myself lumbered with driving.

The friendly locals in this largely Welsh-speaking pub huddle in groups in its numerous nooks and crannies, chatting animatedly, when they're not clogging up the ample bar.

While the pub makes no obvious attempts to attract less mature elements, who prefer thud-thud establishments down the road, many of the younger customers who do gather in the Railway congregate in the sizeable pool room.

There they're deafened by their own juke-box to their hearts' content, which proves nonetheless as unobtrusive in other parts of the establishment as the next train to Amlwch.

Railway Inn, High Street, Llangefni LL77 7NA.
01248 722166

RHOS FYNACH TAVERN,
RHOS ON SEA

THE monks permanently petrified by the entrance stand aside to bid me a warm welcome to their abode.

The Rhos Fynach might not have been a monastery for a great many years, but many's the person who'd swear blind that the monks' ghostly spectres still traipse through the place in their sandals. But then again, it might be something to do with spirits of a completely different kind.

And it's said that buccaneer Henry Morgan – not to be confused with his better known namesake and compatriot who became governor of Jamaica – is another to occasionally still pull up a chair.

Peer into the huge raised fireplace and they say you can see the entrance to the secret tunnels he used to get to the tiny St Trillo's chapel a few hundred yards away by the beach. A wooden bench backing on to the fireplace must have seen countless steaming backs drying out after venturing out along winter's rain-lashed promenade.

The Rhos Fynach – the name translates as the monks' plain or moor – was built in 1181 as a home for the Cistercian monks who earned their keep fishing the weir by Rhos Point to feed their brothers in the larger monastery in Conwy.

It's mentioned in the Charter of Llywelyn ab Iorwerth of 1230, when the monarch also known as Llywelyn the Great sanctioned its purchase by his ally, aristocratic warlord Ednyfed Fychan ap Cynwrig. Evidently even by then it wasn't being used as a monastery.

Sympathetically restored to its former glory in 1990-92, and resembling a medieval house straight off a film set, it's now an aesthetically pleasing pub and restaurant that has reaped some reputation for itself.

Up the handsome, creaking oak staircase you'll find the Monks' Restaurant, licensed for civil weddings, and capable of accommodating up to 70 people. The bar area is open plan but effectively split into three, proudly flashing its impressive bare stone walls and hand-made floor tiles.

On the bar I'm delighted to find the Great Orme Brewery's Orme's Best bitter, brewed just down the road in Glan Conwy. It's a very moreish pint brewed using maris oter malt, but I'm forced to resist the temptation of supping a second one.

The menu similarly has room for local delicacies, which on a typical day might include Conwy plaice or roast Welsh lamb. Today the chalked up specials board includes beef stroganoff and chicken chasseur. The three-course Sunday lunch is a popular weekly feature.

While some of the staff gather around a flashing one-armed bandit, the only other customer in the bar this late afternoon shuffles uncomfortably in his blazer.

We share the silence between us, the sunshine outside still having a bit too much of a nip in it to enjoy the ample *al fresco* facilities at the picnic tables set out on extensive concrete terraces.

Rhos Fynach Tavern, The Promenade, Rhos on Sea LL28 4NG.
01492 548185

SARACENS HEAD,
CERRIGYDRUDION

FOR getting on two centuries the milestone has rested next to Thomas Telford's road linking London to Dublin, battered by extremes of weather on this isolated moorland.

It tells the passer-by that Holyhead is 57 miles in one direction, while in the other it's three miles and two furlongs to Ceirnioge and nine miles and six furlongs to Corwen.

Now better known as the A5, the road has long been an important artery of communication across the wild mountains of north Wales. The Ceirnioge the milestone refers to is Ceirnioge Mawr, the farm down the road where the mail coaches would stop to change horses.

This is Cerrigydrudion, for long a crossroads where lengthy journeys could be broken and weary feet put up over a meal, a cuppa or a pot of ale.

Queen Victoria is said to have stayed the night in Ceirnioge Mawr while on her way to her Irish dominion, while David Lloyd George stayed at the White Lion Inn when heavy snowfall prevented him from making it home to Criccieth. Whether or not he paid the single supplement goes unrecorded!

The Saracens Head Hotel, standing across the road from the stoic milestone, has also long been a welcoming refuge for travellers. And it remains so, being one of few places on a long stretch of road that a passing driver knows with confidence will be open without fail from 8am each day.

As I sup my soft drink to the accompaniment of rolling news blaring somewhat from a forlorn TV set in a far corner near to a pool table, the only other customer sips at his steaming cup of coffee as he peruses his newspaper. But it's only early yet.

The menu tells me that a full-fried breakfast is available between 8am and mid-day, while tantalisingly offering roast meat of the day with vegetables for lunch, or a simple jacket potato. Meanwhile, evening meals are served either in the bar or the sprawling dining area.

The place is welcoming and agriculturally utilitarian, without having been spoilt by the modernisers' hammer, saw and trowel. It features a red quarry-tiled floor in the bar area and a well-trodden carpet elsewhere, with an arched brick fireplace at one end.

It's large enough not to need to be cluttered with a surfeit of furniture, and there's certainly room enough here for the most unsociable to find space for him or herself.

Suddenly another customer makes an appearance, obviously another lone traveller unknown to the barman. He orders a half of Eccleshall's Slaters Original, an ale produced in the outbuildings of the George Inn brewpub in the small Staffordshire town of Eccleshall.

He asks for a menu, flits through it, then promptly downs his beer and disappears through the door. A man obviously in a hurry, without time to enjoy the chill-out effect of the Saracens. It's his loss.

Saracens Head Hotel, Cerrigydrudion LL21 9SY.
01490 420327

SEVEN EYES,
RUTHIN

HIS roof is now fixed a treat, the complete stranger with the distant eyes tells me through a slurred mist. He then compares the virtues of the Magner's Irish cider I've just bought to a more powerful cousin called Jack Frost. He concludes that he prefers Magner's, as he downs the last dregs of his Carlsberg.

I'm rather surprised he isn't wearing the baseball cap offered free with every five pints of Denmark's finest. But then again, it is only 4pm.

Perplexed by the unsolicited information just revealed to me, I sit down at a table engraved with initials, rather like a school desk without the ink stains.

The Seven Eyes, dominating Ruthin's St Peter's Square, is all that a pub should be: unpretentious, roomy, all beams and oak joists, with intriguingly bricked-up former doorways and bare wooden floors. It simply exudes the dusty past.

The pool table is hidden away from the main bar, and the creaking Gothic staircase leads to a first floor cocktail bar, open at weekends. Christopher Lee wouldn't look out of place if he was on the door. No more Bloody Marys for you, sir. But if you're into Moscow Mules and Tequila Sunrises…

Slightly out of sync with this sense of history is the juke-box blaring away, offering everything from 50s and 60s hits to jazz and today's mystifying favourites. Paradoxically it offers a selection of Irish music but nothing Welsh. Disappointingly the open fire in the corner turns out to be fuelled by gas.

Built in the 16th century as a townhouse for Sir Hugh Myddleton, the aristocratic Welsh civil engineer credited with first bringing clean water to London, it was until recent times known as the Myddleton Arms. It was nicknamed the Seven Eyes of Ruthin because of the seven dormer windows that dominate its tiled roof, and has now sensibly adopted that nickname.

Designed by Richard Clough, who'd been trained in Antwerp, it was built in a Dutch style popular through much of what we now know as the Benelux countries.

It's certainly a striking building right in the heart of a market town liberally peppered with medieval masterpieces, and could be straight out of Hans Christian Andersen. One can almost hear the poor princess imprisoned in the attic wailing to her lover below from one of the seven eyes.

Through the huge windows in the bar overlooking the Square I see several black-timbered buildings, built from the rubble that was Ruthin after rebel warlord Owain Glyndŵr razed the town to the ground in 1404, screaming out for my attention.

Study the NatWest Bank across the Square, formerly the local gaol and courthouse, and you might spot the gibbet from which they once hanged local miscreants.

I shiver at the thought. Realising it's time to make my way, I head for the door. The Carlsberg drinker holds it open courteously for me, then stands statuesquely on the pavement wondering which hostelry will next be graced by his presence. The Seven Eyes has that certain ability to knock the senses for six.

Seven Eyes, St Peter's Square, Ruthin LL15 1AA.
01824 707004

SHIP INN,
RED WHARF BAY

THE boats stand on tiptoe above the wide expanse of sand, trying to catch the sun's last warming rays before it sinks into the hillside behind. Casting ever lengthening shadows towards Llanddona some two miles across the bay, the boats submit themselves to the descending twilight and await the return of the tide.

Waders nip between them seeking tasty morsels, while the waves pound at the beach over a mile away awaiting the invitation to flood back in.

Lights flicker into action outside the Ship Inn on the old quayside at Red Wharf Bay, beckoning at the weary traveller. It's difficult to believe this used to be one of the busiest ports on Anglesey's eastern coastline, going back as far as the 15th century. Ships bringing in coal would leave laden with grain or minerals.

It was even a small-scale centre for shipbuilding, eight vessels having been constructed here between 1766 and 1840. Today it's the tourist and his or her pounds, euros and dollars that keeps the village alive.

The Ship was originally known as Cei Bach (Little Quay) and later as the Old Quay, before settling on its present name. It emanates that certain maritime magic, and a Jolly Jack Tar sitting outside sucking on his pipe – banished by the smoking ban – wouldn't go amiss. Indeed I'm surprised to find that a basket hasn't been provided behind the door to park wooden prosthetics in while their owners lean by the bar.

With the door to the bar on the left intriguingly bearing a brass plate marked "H Jones, Dentist", bad memories force me to the other side. Although paying little lip service to the maritime theme, the interior is a cosy olde worlde place, all beamed ceilings and with wooden church pews along the walls.

The menu is extensive and exciting, changing daily, but which could include culinary temptations such as half shoulder of Welsh lamb, fettuccine bolognaise or sea bass with new potatoes.

On the bar I find two cask ales, Adnams and Brains SA, while bottles of Weston's Organic Cider wink for my attention from the fridge. I settle for a pint of my usual fizzy Strongbow.

I head back outside to take in some of the briny evening air. The peace is temporarily desecrated when a boy racer, perhaps a girl racer, decides to demonstrate a certain prowess for inducing wheel-spins on the sands at Llanddona.

A local outside wistfully recalls when another petrolhead once got stuck up to the axles, and wishes the same fate on the social inadequate currently performing.

But what the heck, with views to die for from the armada of tables laid out on the quay and in the beer gardens, why worry about the fate of a floundering pest.

Ship Inn, Red Wharf Bay, Anglesey LL75 8RJ.
01248 852568
www.shipinnredwharfbay.co.uk

TANAT VALLEY INN,
LLANGYNOG

WHEN the pub across the road is dated 1751 and still calls itself the New Inn, its partner the other side of the highway is somehow bound to be wrapped in an antiquity that stretches way back into the mists of time.

And so it proves with the Tanat Valley Inn. It's a 16th century freehouse that would deserve to be dismantled and reassembled in the National History Museum in St Fagan's, were it not still a vibrant part of social life in this ever-so-rural part of Powys. Or Montgomeryshire, as the locals still refer to their often neglected corner of Wales.

The postal address might say Shropshire, Oswestry being but a short drive away and where the local youth invest their money in booze, fags and a good time on a Saturday night. But the locals will unequivocally dispel any doubts that Llangynog is firmly this side of the border.

As I turn the heavy latch on the door, a brass fox's head knocker suspiciously looking me up-and-down as I do so, somebody in the kitchen calls out in Welsh for Anwen's attention. In the compact bar the discourse rumbles on gently in Welsh or English, according to which table I happen to switch my radar into.

The Berwyn mountains huddle around the village, with Bala being an engine-straining drive over that precipitous route across the summit.

This is where on January 23rd, 1974, a mysterious blast up in the mountains and flashing lights in the sky, with the military closing off roads within minutes, led to rumours circulating of an UFO incident still referred to by ufologists as "the Welsh Roswell".

Today the only airborne racket is made by RAF jets shattering the peace and scattering the sheep. Locals prefer to talk more about the price of lambs in Welshpool market than flying saucers.

The "sold out" sign is being stuck on the Cornish-brewed St Austell's Tribute as I approach the bar, while the other real ale appears to be Scotland's Deuchars IPA, maintaining Celtic solidarity. However my fickle taste buds opt to hop just over the border for some Hereford cider.

The servery is as compact as where the clientele has to sit, formality of necessity having to go out of the window in this comfortingly claustrophobic atmosphere. Friendships, however flitting, can hardly fail to be formed drinking in such close proximity.

Another part of the pub, separated from the rest by a short flight of steps, serves as a restaurant area where pub staples such as chicken tikka with rice draws in the punters.

I pop out into the beer garden-cum-car park, where a couple of smokers are dabbing their fags in ancient tin ashtrays carrying the names of long defunct brews Wrexham Lager and Border Bitter. Time, thankfully, still moves slowly in these parts.

Tanat Valley Inn, Llangynog, Powys SY10 0EX.
01691 860227

TAP AND SPILE,
BANGOR

CIGARETTE smoke no longer drifts in great woolly clouds towards the ceiling at the Tap and Spile, but its dappled nicotine-coloured paint wrestles with real nicotine stains for my attention.

The split-level bar is furnished with an eclectic mix of tables, chairs, benches and pews, and has the appearance of what many would expect of a real pub. And while the piano in the corner is unoccupied this late afternoon, this looks the sort of place where the master of the honky-tonk puts his fingers on hold when a stranger moseys in.

As it happens the collection of male drinkers converged around the bar counter, covering a whole range of ages, could hardly be less bothered. While it has its attraction for many of the thousands of students around the city eager to dispose of their loans, the Tap and Spile is also well conversant with bearded imbibers of real ale popping in to mutter into their pints as they peruse their drinking notes.

The stickers on the window indicate that the pub's latest listing in the Good Beer Guide is the umpteenth time it's been included: it's hardly surprising. On tap today are five real ales – Salopian Hop Twister, Deuchars IPA, Adnams, George Wright's King's Ransom and the old faithful that even pubs that don't really cater for the bearded brigade still puts on – Draught Bass.

Not really being a bitter drinker, I wince in embarrassment in ordering a cider, only to be asked by the pleasant young barmaid whether I'd like the fizzy stuff out of an aluminium keg or proper Weston's Old Rosie, without a bubble in sight and at 7.3% ABV strong enough to take the enamel off your teeth. Or words to that effect.

I'm sorely tempted, but I tell the devil whispering in my ear it's way too early to go down Scrumpy Street, much as I'd love to. I reply that, this time, the fizzy stuff will suffice. Well, one does have to look after his good name in the company of complete strangers, you know.

This corner pub has also made for itself a name for its decent if unpretentious nosh, with the specials board today offering plaice and chips or mushroom curry, among other temptations. Another board offers a selection of stotties, with the word on the street warning that a full one can be a challenge even if you've the appetite of a gannet. I desist.

Once called the Garth Hotel, the Tap and Spile stands within earshot of the gulls pestering the walkers taking a bracing walk along Bangor's impressive pier.

It has the feel of a port pub about it, and the views through the windows extend over the browny-grey expanses of the Menai Strait to the posh houses on the opposite shore on Anglesey in what is dubbed Millionaire's Row. I'd much rather be sitting this side, if truth be told.

Tap and Spile, Garth Road, Bangor LL57 2SW.
01248 370835

THE CORN MILL,
LLANGOLLEN

WALKING into the Corn Mill feels very much like being piped aboard a Mississippi paddle steamer run aground on the majestic Dee.

Its outside decks are built directly above the racing rapids below, surely the ultimate in beer garden design, and its warren of cabin-like rooms built on different levels are held up by a forest of beams.

The views over the water to the heritage choo-choos steaming out of the preserved railway station would do Chattanooga proud. Even the water-wheel turning slowly behind the bar has that Deep South feel to it. Huckleberry Finn would have felt very much at home here.

Owned by Brunning and Price, who run a small estate of pubs mostly in north-west England and north-east Wales, the Corn Mill has a long and interesting history.

It was established as a mill by Cistercian monks from Valle Crucis abbey more than seven centuries ago, and it's apparently referred to in a 13th century document about a fishing dispute between the monks and the Freemen of Llangollen.

However the present building is a mere youngster, having stood here since 1786. It was still grinding corn as recently as 1974. It stood empty for many years while its future was debated, much to the locals' consternation, until it opened up in its present guise in 2000.

It has rapidly made a name for itself as a classy venue. As I wander around I encounter people pressed against windows in cosy nooks and crannies everywhere, most of them dining as they relax in the horizontal atmosphere. I could swear I hear the beams creaking as the Dee swells against the foundations.

The menu is huge and changes daily. Today it offers such

delicacies as sweet potato and spinach curry, prawn and haddock risotto and thyme chicken, aubergine, pear and olive salad, or more simple fare like a roast beef sandwich or a brie and grape toastie. Check up on the menu on the pub's website before setting off, so that you'll arrive with your appetite suitably whetted.

Not that the Corn Mill forsakes its role as a purveyor of ales, as too many gastro pubs do. Sure, the wine list is impressive, but no self-respecting beer drinker would find himself or herself at a loss to find something to their taste here.

A number of local imbibers take up their places by the bar, where the ubiquitous choice of lagers and bitters you'd expect in any decent pub await your pleasure.

And the bearded, grumble-bellied brigade need have no fears either, with four real ales on hand-pump, including Conwy Brewery's Honey Fayre. Even red-nosed real cider drinkers are catered for, with Weston's Scrumpy taking up the fifth spot among a quintet of hand pumps. Pardon me, sir? Who needs the Mississippi?

The Corn Mill, Dee Lane, Llangollen LL20 8PN.
01978 869555
www.cornmill-llangollen.co.uk

THE COTTAGE LOAF,
LLANDUDNO

THE man in the Wales T-shirt doesn't even raise his head from the *Daily Post* he's perusing to see who's intruding on his territory as I share his table totally uninvited.

He just spreads his paper further, protecting his terrain as he sups intermittently from his pint of lager. David Attenborough would be fascinated.

But it is a huge wooden table capable of accommodating at least eight, a specimen that wouldn't look out of place in a Bavarian bierkeller, complete with oompah band in lederhosen at its head.

I'm told however that the Cottage Loaf can be anything but the oompah band aficionado's favourite watering-hole on weekend evenings, pulsating to modern music regurgitated at ear splitting levels.

But this lunchtime it's quiet enough, as I sip tentatively at my pint of Conwy Brewery's Castle Bitter, having chosen it over local rival Great Orme Brewery's Orme's Best cask ale for no particular reason. It's comfortingly docile in flavour, and keeps a foamy head to the last dregs.

The silence today is broken only by the murmur of diners' voices and the sharp crackling emanating from the low-slung inglenook fireplace, still insufficient to startle the pair of stone lions lazing either side.

This is a popular stopping-off place with the lunchtime crowd, being right in the centre of town, and an ever-changing menu today includes a Welsh beef dinner, tagliatelle carbonara or a chicken and mayonnaise ciabatta.

Having been a pub only since 1981, converted from an old bakery, the place nonetheless hums of age-old atmosphere, as if it had been welcoming imbibers for centuries.

Set over two levels, the wooden floored top part is more modern in its approach, while down the short flight of steps it's darker and more subdued.

This has a more traditional olde worlde feel to it, set over a stone-flagged floor, with a fine Welsh dresser in one corner, and the whole ceiling held in place by an impressive array of timberwork.

It's said that much of it came from the mast and ribbing of the shipwrecked vessel *Flying Foam*.

Some say it ran aground in 1936, while it could also be the vessel of the same name which sank with the loss of five lives off the County Down coast in 1884 while on its way from Liverpool to Quebec.

Be that as it may, regulars will tell you that the ship's captain – although he survived the disaster, obviously not believing in the adage about going down with your vessel – has taken to haunting the bar area. And especially so when the drink is in full flow!

Quite rightfully boasting it's a village inn in the heart of town, the Cottage Loaf has the added attraction of a sunny south-facing beer terrace to the front and a more extensive area to the rear, complete with a wooden gazebo-style shelter for incurable nicotine addicts.

The Cottage Loaf, Market Street, Llandudno LL30 2SR.
01492 870762
www.the-cottageloaf.co.uk

THE OLD STAG,
LLANGERNYW

THE old place creaks its welcome as I click the latch open and gingerly make my way in. A deafening hush rushes across to embrace me.

Save for the murmuring of two men by the bar, a pin dropping would make sufficient racket to rouse the dead in the ancient churchyard of St Digain's next door.

There's no blaring jukebox; no stroppy flickering TV set demanding infantile attention. The men explain that everybody else has gone to the Bridge to watch this mid-week evening's football match.

Served with my pint of Strongbow, having decided against trying the Timothy Taylor Golden Best that's on hand-pull, I soon merge into the background as the locals return to their chatter. And the talkative barmaid pipes in with tales of her busy young life.

Left to my own devices, I set about on a self-guided tour of this fascinating old freehouse which has served this village in the Clwydian hills between Abergele and Llanrwst since the 17th century.

The bar unassumingly resembles a cross between a bric a brac shop and a museum. Stuffed stag heads and antlers peer at me from nearly every corner, vintage ice skates hang from the heavily adorned beams, age-old swords and shotguns threaten from every angle.

Over there lies the headpiece from a suit of armour, while an old typewriter that would call for fingers of steel to get into action festers angrily, plonked unceremoniously atop a piano stuffed into the entrance to the lounge.

A couple of sofas set either side of a low table are so close to the magnificent inglenook fireplace to suggest it hasn't crackled to the sound of burning logs for some time.

The inn boasts a couple of useful alcoves to hold illicit discussions in, if only I could find someone to hold one with. The snug to the left of the front door offers another refuge from the banter which doubtless rages through the place on busier nights.

And with the Stag enjoying a reputation for its food that stretches way beyond the boundaries of old Denbighshire, it certainly offers many quiet nooks to while away an evening over a meal and a bottle of wine.

Meanwhile, the church of St Digain itself is well worth a visit. It boasts Wales' oldest living specimen – an yew tree reckoned to be at least 4,000 years old – and 7th century pillar stones dating back to the times of the Celtic church.

But it's advised to go along before venturing over the Stag's threshold. History has it that in the past imbibers used to venture into the graveyard on Hallowe'en and press their ears to the church's east window to hear a mysterious spirit intone the names of those destined to pop their clogs in the coming year.

Then, no doubt, they'd head back to the bar to celebrate the good news or drown their sorrows.

The Old Stag, Llangernyw LL22 8PP.
01745 860213

TŶ COCH INN,
PORTH DINLLAEN

RARELY can there be a pub in a more evocative location in the whole of Wales than the Tŷ Coch Inn – the so-called Red House named after the bricks brought in from the Netherlands as ship's ballast that it was built from in 1823.

Often it feels about as Welsh as paella, but it still holds a special place in many Welsh people's hearts, uniquely situated as it is right on Porth Dinllaen's secluded beach on Llŷn's northern coast.

It's one of only two inns in Wales that its patrons have to sail or walk to – the other is in Pembrokeshire. It involves a hike across the beach from Morfa Nefyn or rather more precariously avoiding errant balls over Nefyn's spectacular links golf club.

But on a warm summer's day or a balmy evening it's well worth the effort, shaking the sand that sweeps up to the doorway from your feet before making your entrance.

Surely shouldn't 'Desert Island Discs' be broadcast every week from the cosy single bar, with its brass and maritime paraphernalia? With the lulling lap of the waves just feet away, piped music would do it a grave injustice and the pub is mostly filled with idle chatter of the most laid-back manner. But ghostly strains of sea shanties of old still pervade the fabric of the place.

I'm almost tempted to ask for the whereabouts of that old seadog Capt. Huw Puw that J. Glyn Davies wrote about in the most famous Welsh sea shanty of all, 'Fflat Huw Puw', which he set in Porth Dinllaen. One can almost hear his men splicing the mainbrace before setting off for corners of the world far removed from here, yet unlikely to match anything Porth Dinllaen has to offer.

It was once a bustling ship-building centre earmarked as the main Irish Sea port before Holyhead beat it to it. Some 60 boats still bob and clank in the bay as we settle by the wall outside to enjoy the ambience, the clientele a mixture of young locals chatting in Welsh and others from further afield chatting in English. The peace is only once shattered by a pillock on a pillion roaring his motorbike along the beach.

Landlady Brione Webley runs a tight ship at the Tŷ Coch. Junk food you won't get, and just don't even think about asking for chips. In fact if you want a meal at all it'll have to be in the daytime.

Understandably, given its isolated location and the relative lack of locals who live in the immediate vicinity, the Tŷ Coch is largely a summer pub. After October it restricts its opening hours to Saturday afternoons and occasional Sunday lunchtimes, where walkers can warm their backsides by the roaring fire after a bracing stroll through the winter elements.

Beer might cost you well in excess of other pubs in the locality, real ale aficionados have to make do with bottled stuff, and the toilets might be outside, with the gents' urinals even out in the open air. But this is still one unique pub that just has to be worth a visit.

Tŷ Coch Inn, Porth Dinllaen, near Nefyn LL53 6DB
01758 720498
www.tycoch.co.uk

SUN INN,
LLANENGAN

A SLIGHT chill sets in as the evening sun dips behind Mynydd Rhiw, sending a cooling zephyr through the trembling hedgerows. The tall chimney stack of a long-disused lead mine casts rapidly lengthening shadows scuttling across the ochre hillside above.

Our minds are made up for us, as we skirt around an otherwise engaging beer garden and partly covered patio trying its utmost to entice us into its lonely embrace.

We pass up the offer, heading indoors, but making a mental note to get here before sunset the next time we're in these parts.

This is Llanengan in deepest rural Llŷn, more of an over-grown hamlet than a village in many respects.

The twittering of the birds only have the tinkling of silver streams to compete with for much of the time, even given that brash, noisy and thoroughly alien Abersoch is barely more than five minutes away by tractor. Chelsea tractor, that is.

One of those infernal contraptions, the lack of agricultural deposits indicating its urban origins rather than being a necessary farmer's tool, blocks up the capillary-tight main lane. Its dipstick driver fails to recognise the need to occasionally reverse in these parts, from a matter of practicality and courtesy.

Observing this two-vehicle traffic jam through the wide expanses of the bay windows, I take our drinks and a menu from the bar to a table in the heavily wood-panelled lounge.

This being a Robinsons house, it is naturally strictly tied in the drinks it can offer, sadly having to eschew the opportunity to offer more local ales, wines and spirits. The green brigade, not to mention the grumble-bellies that love real ale, must be tearing their hair out at this lost opportunity.

The cask beers on offer therefore seem restricted to Robinson's own perfectly palatable in-house Unicorn and Top Tipple brands.

This room is set out over two levels, separated by only a couple of steps with coffee and condiments stations either side.

The locals seem to prefer the more utilitarian public bar the other side, reached by a couple of doors either side of the servery, offering a circuit with which to perpetually escape from the pub bore.

This carpeted room we're in resounds to accents and even language far removed from that which fits in more naturally here.

It's accentuated by a total lack of any background music, which would've helped matters along in those rare moments when they've exhausted regaling the whole establishment and half the village with their tales of derring-do on the knee-deep high seas.

Most of them are seemingly here for the food more than a drink. And the Sun certainly has earned its spurs down the years, among both the jet-skiing Chelsea set in Abersoch and the locals.

The menu is mercifully not over-elaborate and certainly offers something for all tastes, including perennial pub favourites such as sirloin steak and fish pie.

Sun Inn, Llanengan, near Pwllheli LL53 7LG.
01758 712660

VICTORIA INN,
LLANBEDR

BUILT more for the horse and cart than tourist coaches and caravans towed by numbskulls in Chelsea tractors, the A496 takes a deep intake of breath and sucks in its ribcage as it squeezes its way through Llanbedr.

This forces the passing hordes motoring through between Harlech and Barmouth to at least take in what this sliver of a village has to offer. While you won't find your baker or candlestick-maker, you'll find your butcher, your restaurant, your local Spar and a top-notch delicatessen which you'll be hard pressed to better anywhere along the Cardigan Bay coast.

Then, directly across the road, the scowling face of Prince Albert's other half – trademark veil over her head – does her level best, from her vantage point on the swinging name sign above the front door, to dissuade you from entering the ancient coaching inn named after her.

The Victoria Inn is another of Stockport brewers' Frederic Robinson's Welsh estate, with the ubiquitous Unicorn cask ale coming in its wake. The place simply seeps history: we disregard Her Majesty's Teutonic glower and make our way in.

The place has in recent times undergone a revamp, giving it a light and airy feel, but we still head for welcoming familiarity of the Settle Bar.

It's named after the intriguing ancient circular wooden settle, where a young couple are canoodling, protected to some degree from prying eyes by its tall wooden back.

It faces an original stove, standing in the centre like a story-teller about to embark on another load of baloney, and it's where the drivers off the stagecoaches would undoubtedly have stood on the stone-flagged floor to dry their steaming rear ends as they supped their ale.

Another coaching tradition here is that of accommodation, although all the bedrooms these days are *en suite* and fully centrally heated.

Since local accents, language and customs were largely superseded in this part of Meirionnydd, it's become increasingly difficult to tell tourists and locals apart. The two elderly gentlemen in cardigans chatting over their pint pots, the only other denizens of the Settle Bar this early evening, could be either I suppose.

The surrounding countryside has much to commend it for those seeking a day out in the bracing fresh air, or a longer break away from it all.

The Victoria boasts it's within easy reach of fishing, golf, pony trekking, water sports, climbing and walking. Which all seems a rather strenuous form of relaxation to me. I decide I'd rather spend a lazy afternoon in the spacious beer garden with a good book and something cold between my lips, were the option ever to come up.

With that we sup the last dregs of our drinks. Her Majesty, though, is still not the least bit amused as we leave. No wonder her better half popped his clogs first.

Victoria Inn, Llanbedr, near Harlech LL45 2LD.
01341 241213
www.vic-inn.co.uk

WHITE HORSE INN,
CAPEL GARMON

NOT even an owl stirs nor a dog barks in the village as the White Horse basks in the chill limelight of a moon almost in full bloom. But then again, we are some 800 feet above sea level here in Capel Garmon, in the hills that clamber up the Conwy Valley just a couple of miles above the tourist honey-pot that is Betws-y-coed.

The pair of concrete horses' heads at the entrance to the car park stubbornly refuse to acknowledge my presence, while the deserted picnic tables hark back to warmer times when ample bottoms warmed up their now shivering timbers.

Popular with walkers and ramblers, and a place to chill out for holidaymakers seeking to escape the suffocating hordes of fellow tourists that throng Betws' pubs in the summer, the views from here are to kill for. They are, if anything, accentuated viewed by moonlight.

Not one for using tradesmen's entrances, I decide against using the back door and head for the front.

The White Horse stands on a sharp bend on the narrow lane leading through the village, opposite an old shop full of village character that seems to have long since pulled down the shutters.

The metal mailbox and the traditional red telephone kiosk standing to attention next to it indicate that it would at one time have been the post office, an important centre for village gossip and social interaction.

I depress the latch on the pub's tightly shut wooden door, only half expecting it to open, and its loud click echoes through the place as I gingerly make my way inside.

Just a couple of heads turn in the bar this early evening to inspect this stranger in town, but they soon settle down again to watch the news from Cardiff on the huge TV screen on the far wall next to a pool table.

I assume that this is the public bar, an immaculately maintained room that's spotlessly clean and dazzlingly white, with a real fire crackling away in one corner and countless mugs dangling lazily from black-painted beams.

This inn has been part of village life in these parts since the 16th century, and now stands as one of the last bastions against a total shutdown in rural services. A comprehensive price list of confectionery pinned behind the bar indicates that the place doubles up as the local tuck shop.

This is reputedly where former Tory leader William Hague – Mr 14 Pints a Day – met his wife-to-be Ffion, but don't let that put you off.

It's dotted with settles full of country character and has oodles of atmosphere, even if a little less illumination wouldn't go amiss, and has a deserved reputation among tourists and locals alike for its nightly food offering.

The menu is extensive and interesting, while the specials board this evening includes plain and simple pub staples such as liver and onions and sausage and mash.

White Horse Inn,
Capel Garmon, near Betws-y-coed LL26 0RW.
01690 710271

WHITE LION INN,
LLANELIAN-YN-RHOS

THE Welsh clergy and the inn have often been at loggerheads: it would however be difficult for churchgoers and indulgers in rather more than the odd sip of communion wine not to engage with each other in Llanelian-yn-Rhos.

The church of St Elian and the White Lion Inn stand cheek to jowl, worshippers stepping from the churchyard sharing the same cobbled courtyard as imbibers basking in the sun in the pub's beer garden.

Indeed the tiny snug on your right as you step into the inn, capable of holding no more than half a dozen close acquaintances within its sardine-tin confines, is known for offering liquid sustenance after Sunday service to those of the dog-collared profession who'd rather not step into the limelight of the pub proper.

Stretching like a lazy cat high on the hillside on the outskirts of Colwyn Bay, looking out over the twinkling azure spread of the Irish Sea below, little has changed in Llanelian down the decades. Centuries, even.

In 1699 noted naturalist, botanist, linguist, geographer and antiquary Edward Lhuyd wrote of the village: "There are by ye church but four or five houses". In the following three centuries that number has spiralled to 18.

The building which nowadays houses the White Lion, named after the lion rampant coat-of-arms of the local landowning Holland dynasty, would've been at least 300 years old in Lhuyd's time.

However tradition has it that as far back as 722 AD the church elders – the first church in Llanelian having been erected in the 6th century – would make their way to "the ale house next door" for their customary free ale. Times, however, move on. Nowadays they have to pay for it.

Three ladies stand outside in their jodhpurs, gripping tightly on their horses' reins with one hand and sipping soft drinks with the other. A stirrup cup would not go amiss. Meanwhile the horses, eager to get on their way, quietly neigh their disgust.

The inn itself is a gem, an L-shaped place where jugs, glasses, pots and teapots dangle cavalierly from beams, as if threatening to jump and dashing themselves to smithereens on the slate floor below.

Populated by an eclectic mix of furniture, settles, chairs and luxurious leather Chesterfields, the bar also boasts the inglenook fireplace requisite of any inn worth its architectural salt.

Noted among real ale aficionados, today it has two Marstons' ales on hand-pull, Pedigree and Burton Ale. But this lunchtime most appear to be indulging in little more than soft drinks as they order meals.

The White Lion offers the whole gamut, from sandwiches to the full menu. The specials board tantalisingly beckons like a tart in a bordello window, with home-made mousakka or Edwards of Conwy's pork and leek sausages with mash threatening to turn a short stop-over into an extended stay.

White Lion Inn,
Llanelian-yn-Rhos,
near Colwyn Bay
LL29 8YA.
01492 515807
www.whitelioninn.co.uk

WHITE LION,
TALYBONT

MANY years might have passed since I last stumbled out of the White Lion, but some things never change.

The entrance to the public bar remains unmarked, and half a dozen heads swing round to see who's making an appearance as we tentatively delve back into the muddied mists of time and opt to push open the door on the right.

They immediately launch into some sort of Welsh Inquisition – who, where from and why? I'm tempted to stick to name, rank and number, until it becomes obvious they intend to charm the information out of us rather than reaching for the branding irons.

I'm soon informed that the last time I was in here was back in 1992. I must have made quite an impression. Or it might be that I let it slip that it was when the National Eisteddfod last visited Aberystwyth.

The bar is a cosy sort of place where you'd expect to see a pack of farmers in caked wellington boots crowding around the burner in the fireplace with barbecuing backsides. Except that none of these look like farmers.

The Banks' ales that are a feature of many pubs in these parts seems to be going down a treat. Meanwhile rows of empty half litre bottles of Wychcraft Blonde Beer from the Wychwood Brewery in Oxfordshire standing to attention on one of the tables suggests that one tippler is very happy with life's lot.

Fitted with rustic wooden settles and a bric-a-brac mix of furniture sitting on an original slate flagged floor, the U-shaped room is light and airy. Metal hooks in the ceiling indicate the place was once a butcher's shop.

The piano in the bar is a rare commodity these days. It suggests that the entertainment here is more of the traditional home-grown variety than overpaid pub acts, often little more than glorified karaoke performers singing to pre-recorded backing tracks that make them sound as if they're accompanied by full orchestras.

The back bar is unlit this early evening, but in the brooding gloom I can still make out that it too has a similar mix of furniture, including a wooden settle. The gents' toilet is rather eccentrically candle-lit as I inspect it, adding even further to the place's quaintly Ruritanian feel.

This is one of two pubs in the village, the other being immediately next door and named the Black Lion. So there's no friendly competition there, then! Both overlook the ancient village green where fairs have traditionally been held.

The White Lion has earned quite a reputation for its food, served either in the bars, in its own dedicated dining room or out in the front overlooking the green and the traffic snaking past between Machynlleth and Aberystwyth.

Sea food has long been a speciality, while it also boasts of its use of Welsh reared meats, with the sirloin and the gammon steak old favourites.

White Lion Hotel, Talybont, Ceredigion SY24 5ER.
01970 832245

YR HEN LEW DU,
ABERYSTWYTH

UNIVERSITY towns on the whole have their student pubs, and their pubs for the rest of humanity. Yr Hen Lew Du in Bridge Street, little more than a minute's staggering time from Aberystwyth's main drag, manages somehow to be all things to all men, women and the undecided.

Sure, this early 18th century inn is popular among the student set, and particularly so among the sizeable minority at the town's University of Wales who actually hail from all corners of Wales. But the locals love popping in as well.

A middle-aged couple are scraping at their spotlessly-clean plates in the tiny bar on the left as I enter, he speaking in Welsh while she interrupts him in English in that paradoxically rural attempt at being urbanised that Aber likes to indulge in.

Just feet away a young couple are engaged in eye-fluttering lovey-dovey talk in a distinctly northern dialect of Welsh, making their meal last as long as possible. It's not that I'm given to eavesdropping, just that the room is so confined that Beethoven would have difficulty in not picking up on the odd secret.

The furniture seems to have been shoved in indiscriminately on to the stone-flagged floor straight off the back of a van. The wooden beams are painted in an utilitarian shade of green not often seen these days outside of heritage railways' loco sheds.

Mind you, with the huge all-day breakfast costing a pittance and gammon and chips little more, evidently targeting the penny-pinching student market, who could complain if you're virtually sitting on your fellow diners' laps?

Not that the pub in itself is small. Anything but. It's a rambling rabbit warren of a place, all bare wooden floors and deliciously dark nooks and crannies where giggling students discuss their latest conquests while supping insipid Irish cider tipped over distinctly Welsh ice.

Their tastes are further catered for by the Coors, Grolsch and the ubiquitous and tasteless Carling Extra Cold on the bar. A cash machine flashes that colourful plastic grin through the darkness as it invites them to add to that student loan debt, no doubt charging something in the order of £2.50 to save them the hassle of tramping through the rain to their bank's free hole-in-the-wall all of 300-yards away.

Meanwhile a trio of young females are murdering one of evergreen Meic Stevens' classic ballads while perched precariously on their bar stools, their rasping tones echoing off the bare walls.

How I could have killed for some decent weather to sit at the tables on the stone-pitched forecourt outside.

In summer you can sit there drinking in the petrol fumes while sneering at boy racers as they enter their 74th lap around the town centre.

Most of the year, though, it's Stevens impersonations or getting soaked to the skin. Stevens wins by a mile. I sup harder in an effort to accentuate my deafness.

Yr Hen Lew Du, Bridge Street, Aberystwyth SY23 1PZ.
01970 615378